W9-BUH-553

The Reasoning Heart

TOWARD A NORTH AMERICAN THEOLOGY

The Reasoning Heart

TOWARD A NORTH AMERICAN THEOLOGY

FRANK M. OPPENHEIM, S.J.
Editor

Georgetown University Press
Washington, D.C.

Cover art: Matisse, Henri (1869-1954) Icare. (Icarus) Plate 8 from
Jazz. Paris, published by Tériade, 1947. Copyright © 1983 By The
Metropolitan Museum of Art, Gift of Lila Acheson Wallace, 1983.
(1983.1009)

These essays originally appeared in *Theological Studies*, and are used with permission.

Copyright © 1982, 1983, 1984 by Theological Studies
Introduction Copyright © 1986 by Georgetown University Press
All Rights Reserved
Printed in the United States of America

Library of Congress Cataloging-in-Publication Data

The Reasoning heart.

  Result of the work of the John Courtney Murray
Writer's Group and originally appeared in Theological
studies.
  Includes index.
  Contents: Faith's adventure—an overview/Drew
Christiansen—Conversion—the challenge of contemporary
charismatic piety/Donald Gelpi—The reasoning heart—
an American approach to Christian discernment/William
Spohn—[etc.]
  1. Theology. I. Oppenheim, Frank M., 1925-
II. John Courtney Murray Writers' Group (U.S.)
III. Theological studies (Baltimore, Md.)
BT80.R36 1986   230   86-4655
ISBN 0-87840-439-2
ISBN 0-87840-433-3 (pbk.)

Contents

DREW CHRISTIANSEN

Faith's Adventure: An Overview

DREW CHRISTIANSEN, S.J., is professor of Christian social
ethics at the Jesuit School of Theology in Berkeley, California. He has contributed articles to the *Encyclopedia of
Bioethics*, and various scholarly journals; his chapter "Basic
Needs: Criteria for the Legitimacy of Development" appeared in *Human Rights in the Americas: The Struggle for
Consensus*.

Wallace Stevens, in a poem entitled "To An Old Philosopher in Rome," a memorial to the American thinker George Santayana who passed his last years in the Eternal City, captured the spirit of American religious philosophy in four lines of verse:

> A light on the candle tearing against the wick
> To join a hovering excellence, to escape
> From Fire and be part only of that of which
> Fire is the symbol: the celestial possible.[1]

Stevens's verses reflect the distinctive accent of the classical American philosophers, for they regarded possibility as a foretaste of beatitude. In possibility they felt the living presence of God at work in human history. The essays gathered in this volume likewise share a common conviction that God is living and active in our lives through our sense of the possible. God renews our life like the eagle's. For those who are moved by God's stirrings, the life of faith is an adventure. In the pages that follow, my role will be to provide an orientation of sorts for the explorations of religious ideas found in the work of the John Courtney Murray Writers' Group and the American thinkers who have inspired them. The members of the group are Jesuits Donald Gelpi, John Mueller, Frank Oppenheim, William Spohn and John Stacer. The uniqueness of the group's program is to appropriate resources in American philosophy for the development of a North American theology.

My purpose in this introduction is to present a synthetic overview. I will endeavor to show how each author contributes a distinctively American perspective to the interpretation of religious experience and the religious depths of American culture. They draw on the classic authors of the American tradition: Peirce, James, Royce, Dewey and Hocking in religious philosophy, and Edwards, H. R. Niebuhr and Meland in philosophical theology. Like these classical American thinkers, they elaborate theologies which are affective and aesthetic in the interpretation of religion and pragmatic in their concern for the moral and social applications of theology. In so doing, they make a special contribution to ecumenical theology, linking perduring themes in Catholic theology and spirituality, like community and discernment, with the experiential tra-

---

[1] Wallace Stevens, *Collected Poems* (New York: Alfred Knopf, 1957), 515.

1

dition of American frontier Protestantism. They also lay the groundwork
for a dialogue with religious humanism where the categories of philosophical analysis have grown, as in the case of John Dewey or Josiah
Royce, out of the soil of living religious traditions and yet taken on a life
of their own. In this many-sided dialogue, the Murray Group offers fresh
avenues of inquiry for Church practice on the part of American Catholics
as well, with new appreciations of basic Christian experiences like conversion, grace and sacrament.

The Murray Group program is noteworthy because of its use of classic
American philosophies rather than imported styles of theological inquiry
borrowed from Europe or more recently from Latin America. On the
whole, Protestant thinkers have been more original in adapting to the
American context than Catholic theologians. While Protestantism has
also had schools of thought enormously dependent on European theology—one thinks of Liberalism in the late nineteenth century and Bar-
thianism and Neo-Orthodoxy in the mid-twentieth century—American
Protestantism has also produced a number of schools of thought which
have had distinctively American features. In this century alone, there
have been Walter Rauschenbusch and the Social Gospelers, Reinhold
Niebuhr and the Christian Realists, H. Richard Niebuhr and the Ethics
of Responsibility. Each worked out a theology which responded to characteristically American questions, drew on American sources and experiences, and employed new vocabularies and models of thought. The only
Catholic theologian of equal originality was John Courtney Murray.

Murray addressed typically American questions like religious liberty,
church and state, law and ethics; but even he did not draw in any
significant way on the American intellectual tradition in his writings.
While the United States, with its system of Catholic institutions of
higher education, has become one of the leading centers for theological
education in the Catholic world, American Catholic theologians have still
made very few moves to appropriate the American tradition in their
writings. Most still turn to Europe for intellectual leadership, and a
smaller, but stimulating group look to liberation theology for inspiration.
The novelty of the Murray Group to which these five authors belong is
that it has chosen to utilize resources from the tradition of American
religious philosophy in elaborating contemporary theologies of its own.
It consciously places itself in the tradition of religious thought begun in
the eighteenth century with the Puritan divine Jonathan Edwards. It
continues reasoned reflection on religious experience, religious affections
and religious belief in the spirit of Edwards.

The classics of American philosophy share an important feature of
religious inquiry with Catholic thought. Both traditions see continuity

between lived experience, philosophy and theology. While the American tradition, like American churches, is emphatically experiential, the major thinkers have not sustained the opposition between experience and divine revelation, which was so much a part of Reformation theology. Thus, American religious philosophy offers a fresh look at the experience of Christian faith in this country freed of traditional confessional polemics.

Moreover, even when it has taken a secular turn as in the work of George Santayana and John Dewey, American philosophy has shown exceptional interest in religion. Thinkers like Peirce, James and Royce showed a concern, exceptional among modern philosophers, not only with religious questions but with religious traditions. They were convinced that human experience could not be properly comprehended without use of the store of ideas and perceptions which Christianity bequeathed to Western civilization. James, for example, found in the practice of voluntary poverty, the paradigm for "the moral equivalent of war." Peirce took Love (Agape) to be a primary metaphysical category; and Royce found in the church of universally loyal persons the fullest realization of human community.

At the same time American philosophers have reflected on religious experience, their theological counterparts have shown an enthusiasm for philosophical modes of reasoning not often shared by American Protestant Churches with their customary biblicist and confessional styles of thought. Jonathan Edwards's *Dissertation on the Nature of True Virtue*, for example, combines an experiential approach to faith with elements of Platonic and Scholastic reasoning. H. Richard Niebuhr in his influential book *The Responsible Self* employed themes and concepts from Josiah Royce and the social philosopher and psychologist George Herbert Mead. Niebuhr, not unlike his Catholic contemporaries Etienne Gilson and Jacques Maritain, also preferred to call himself a "Christian moral philosopher" rather than a theologian. This openness to philosophy as a tool for religious inquiry, on the one hand, with philosophical exploration of religion, on the other, makes the American classics an exceptionally fruitful field for ecumenical rapprochement with theologians in the Catholic tradition, where the connections between human experience, philosophy and theology have repeatedly been affirmed. At the same time, the opportunity to explore those connections through the eyes of American philosophy offers Catholic theologians fresh perspectives from which to examine the Catholic tradition.

AMERICAN RELIGIOUS PHILOSOPHY

American religious philosophy, as understood by our five authors, is distinguished by four characteristic traits. It is (1) experiential, (2) affective, (3) aesthetic and (4) pragmatic. Unlike Continental philosophy, which has tended to rationalism, and recent British philosophy, which has sometimes reduced itself to an academic exercise in verbal analysis, the American tradition has tended not only to draw on experience, but even, as in the case of John Dewey, to make experience a fundamental category of philosophical analysis. The result has been a philosophy informed directly and indirectly by a wide range of human activities. Royce's philosophy of community, for example, grew out of his reaction to the individualism of the California Gold Rush country where he grew up. Edwards's *Treatise on the Religious Affections* stemmed from his own involvement in the Great Awakening. Whitehead took the whole sweep of Western history and institutions as the data for his philosophy of civilization. James examined "the varieties of religious experience." Dewey's articulation of a "a common faith" was continuous with his experiments in educational and social reform. Human life in its rich personal, institutional, cultural, political and religious variety is the subject matter for American philosophy.

"Experience" also provides for the American tradition a distinctive method of philosophical reflection. Experience is the organizing principle for American thought the way reason has been for Continental European thought. Experience is the comprehensive category which embraces reason and the affections, order and novelty, tradition and innovation. With experience as the integrating factor, reason and the affections interrelate, each serving to clarify the other, as people try to understand the human condition and to improve their situations of life. In this sense, experience as a method is not simply a passive reporting of established patterns and trends. It is itself experimental, trying new possibilities, testing new ways of life. At this level, religion is vitally important, leading humanity into its future both by the light of ideas and the lure of feeling.

The affections also play an important part in American religious philosophy. They are neither unruly desires nor secondary phenomena subordinate to rational controls. They are co-equal with reason, possess a logic of their own, and themselves serve a cognitive function. At the same time, they unite in feeling what reason divides. If intelligence without well-ordered affection is mere cleverness, American religious philosophy represents humane rationality, because the affections set the context in which reason can be at play.

The prominence of the affections in American thought makes it easy to anticipate a fruitful exchange with those strands of the Catholic theological tradition, such as the Augustinian school and monastic and spiritual theology, which have maintained an emphasis on affective knowledge. Contemporary students of Hans Urs von Balthasar may also find here an important resource for reaching American audiences. But American philosophy has something to teach Catholic theology too. It offers a far more explicit and developed understanding of the logic of emotion than the classical tradition on which Catholic theology has depended. Moreover, it has a firmer grasp of the connection between action and affection than is customarily found in Catholic spirituality and ethics. There is much here to be explored.

Third, American religious philosophy and particularly theology, as found in Edwards and Niebuhr, for example, is aesthetic in character. Beauty has played a unifying role in American philosophy. In reflection on the moral life, beauty has served to unite the right and the good. It has also provided a way to understand the unity of diverse values by an appeal to Divine Beauty. Jonathan Edwards gave the lead for this aesthetic theology in *Religious Affections* and *The Nature of True Virtue*. The only virtuous moral acts, Edwards argued, are ones which fit our moral intentions into the comprehensive affirmation of the beauty of Being.

The aesthetic dimension in American moral philosophy sees unity in human experience by seeing the part within the whole. Hocking and Whitehead, for example, insisted on seeing any single entity or action as an event within a comprehensive process of emergent meaning. In *The Meaning of Revelation*, H. R. Niebuhr sees theological reasoning as fundamentally the relating of parts to the whole. He holds that we humans require a narrative unity to provide a sense of the whole for our personal and communal experience. In *The Responsible Self*, where he argues that root metaphors shape our self-interpretation and guide our moral discernment, Niebuhr argues that "we interpret the things that force themselves upon us as parts of wholes, as related and as symbolic of larger meanings."[2]

From Edwards to Niebuhr, therefore, the American tradition is marked by an aesthetic way of reasoning. It holds that we do not abstract universal features from particular experience, so much as we recognize their significance in an aesthetic pattern. We locate them as parts to wholes, as we search for the more comprehensive frameworks of meaning that will enable experiences to disclose their fullest significance. Although Edwards's aesthetics drew on a Platonic epistemology of participation, Royce's on human needs and ideals and Niebuhr's on literary categories, all can be said to express an aesthetic perspective on experience and morality. For all, that action is both right and good which fits harmoniously into the comprehensive whole of meaning.

Accordingly, the aesthetic dimension of American thought is a corollary

[2] H. R. Niebuhr, *The Responsible Self* (New York: Harper and Row, 1963), 61–62.

to the affective dimension. As James instructed us, feelings grasp a sense of the whole situation, they give a synthetic glimpse of integrated value and truth. The responsible agent strives to discern the fitting action through a logic of affectivity by locating the partial action within the comprehensive whole. Harmony rather than deductive rigor, therefore, characterizes this aesthetic religious ethics. Even if the language differs, Catholic moralists will recognize in this a certain kinship with Aquinas's "knowledge by connaturality."

Fourth, the American tradition is pragmatist. The names of Peirce, James and Dewey, of course, are associated with Pragmatism as a school of philosophy. But concern for action, particularly social action, is a characteristic of other classic American thinkers as well. Edwards's theology is concerned with conversion. Royce's mature thought arises from "modes of action" and leads on into further ones. Niebuhr's ethics, like Whitehead's process thought and cultural philosophy, envisages life as continuous interaction. Furthermore, what is distinctive about American philosophy is that human action produces novelty. God's presence is felt as much in the movement to the future as in the revelations of the past. To Catholics, who since Pope John XXIII and Vatican II have become accustomed to reading the "signs of the times," the orientation of American thought to the future should be a useful resource for further theological inquiry. Whether it is Richard Niebuhr asking what God is doing in history or Whitehead tracing the lure of the divine ideas in civilization, American philosophy provides ways for understanding the movement of humankind into the future as essentially a religious experience. The interaction between the nascent theology of the post-Vatican II Church and American religious philosophy, therefore, not only offers potential for elaborating an American Catholic theology, but also, and perhaps more significantly for the universal Church, provides ways of understanding our faith in terms of the Spirit's action in humankind's passage through history.

Finally, a brief word about the distinctive religious accents of American philosophy. Transformation, both personal and social, is a primary theme in the American classics. There are echoes of the Great Awakening and nineteenth-century revivalist camp meetings. Conversion is a key religious symbol. Even though there is here a high level of moral awareness and purpose, Americans tend to look on moral conversion as arising from affective and aesthetic moments of life rather than from acts of will or intellect. Similarly, morality is found not so much in the single act as in a wholeness of life and patterns of action. It is part and whole again. In the same way, while one must make exceptions for the individualism of Transcendentalism and William James, American religious thought generally tends to see religious life in social terms. It places the individual in community, and it values the great religious traditions for doing the same.

Religion as seen by the classic American philosophers is not a religion of aloof mystery. American theology, in this sense, does not study the divine-in-itself. It is "empirical," verifying its convictions in history, and testing them in conduct. It examines how the divine affects human life. In its empiricism, it tends to neglect the traditional sources of theology: bible, doctrine, the church. Instead, at one and the same time it trusts in the immediacy of experience and shows a willingness to accept mediation in nature and history rather than through ecclesiastical institutions. This empirical religion has both its losses and its gains, but I shall not expound on either here.

For American Catholics, the importance of the religious philosophy found in the American philosophical classics lies first off in a native idiom which has many of the same accents as the Catholic tradition: the unity of reason and affection, the movement of desire, an aesthetic vision of life, a social conception of human nature. Second, American religious philosophy suggests ways in which a native theology can be critical of the culture from which it emerges. Latin American liberation theology has given a critique of culture and politics in that region; political theology, as found in the work of J-B. Metz, provides a critical analysis of bourgeois European society. But mainline American Catholic theologians have yet to develop a sustained critique of our culture and its institutions. The American classics provide models of how that might be done in keeping with many of the dominant strains of American culture. Third, American religious philosophy puts Catholic theologians in contact with some of the recurrent forms of American religious experience, with conversion and revival, with moral reformism and political activism. In so doing, it provides the background for a theology which responds to typically American forms of faith. Finally, in its accent on action as the fruit of faith and novelty as God's work in history—as well as ours— classic American philosophy draws on strains in the American experience which may well be fertile themes for incorporation into the Catholic tradition.

A SYNTHETIC OVERVIEW

Rather than provide a standard introductory essay, summarizing the five pieces published here and drawing connections among them, I have, at the urgings of the contributors and Frank Oppenheim, our editor, written instead a synthetic overview from yet another perspective, the thought of Alfred North Whitehead. Whitehead was a transplanted Englishman who wrote nearly all his philosophical corpus during his tenure from 1924 to 1937 as professor of philosophy at Harvard University. Whitehead's influence on American philosophy and theology has been as great as that of any single thinker. He is best known as the founding father of process philosophy and theology. But, rather than drawing on the more abstract categories of process thought, I turn to Whitehead's philosophy of civilization, in which religion plays a supremely important role, to provide a perspective from which to introduce the essays in this volume. An overview from the perspective of Whitehead's philosophy of civilization is congenial to the work of our authors, because like their own essays it never gets far from primary religious experiences and their expression in rituals, institutions and culture. With them it shares the characteristics of American religious philosophy as experiential, affective, aesthetic and pragmatic. But most importantly, it shows how faith is the force that propels humankind through history.

Originally, this chapter was prepared as a summary article for what was projected as a single special issue of *Theological Studies*. As it turned out, the essays appeared over many months in five separate issues of *Theological Studies*. For that reason, the summary was not needed. So, it appears here for the first time, revised as an introduction. Since it works from a special perspective of its own, it is probably better to think of it as a synthetic overview than as an introduction in the usual sense. As an overview, it highlights themes common to all the essays in this volume. As a synthesis, it focuses this material in a distinctive way of its own, namely, the adventure of faith.

The essay consists of three parts: (1) an explanation of Whitehead's views of cultural renewal; (2) the application of these theories to the project of doing an inculturated American theology; and (3) reflections on how each of the articles in this series has contributed to an American theology with practical implications for the renewal of the American Church and American society.

1. Religion and Societal Renewal

The proposal made by the members of the Murray Group that the classic American philosophers may serve as a font for the rejuvenation of theology in this country comes at an appropriate time. In Church circles, there has long been discontent with the reliance of teachers of theology on European and more recently Latin American models, and efforts to generate an indigenous theology have yet to have notable results. At the same time, cultural commentators of all stripes are showing considerable interest in renewal of morality in Western society and appear to appreciate the importance of religion in that revival. Some secular thinkers have even begun to suspect that societal decay can be reversed only by a morality which has the conviction of religion to give it strength.[3] On the part of certain nonbelievers, this turn to religion may be merely a fond hope, an unconscious nostalgia for a faith they have never known. On the part of others, it may even be interpreted more cynically as a malign manipulation of popular credulity for the convenience of our governors. However we interpret the recent appreciation for religion among secular thinkers, the fact remains that there is renewed interest in religion as a source of moral and cultural rejuvenation.

Unfortunately, all too often the mistake of pundits and of groups like the Moral Majority is to look behind them to the past as the exclusive source of inspiration. They seek to restore customs and values which justify the present disposition of economic and political interests without meeting any of the deeper moral perplexities of the culture, condemning its failures, or challenging the people and their rulers to repentance. They rely on a ritualistic repetition of discarded formulas to bring about change; but their formulas lack the power to persuade.

Persuasion requires more than nostalgia for order and simplicity. It demands a sense of direction. Discipline must carry with it the promise of a fuller life, and the allegiances of faith require devotion to wider purposes capable of expanding the soul. The pertinence of American philosophy not only to the development of an indigenous theology but also to the broader debate over the future of American society is that it provides a perspective on history in which religion plays a decisive role, not just as conservator of the past but as pioneer of the future. From the beginnings of recorded history, religion has provided the impetus for profound social change. For this reason, it is not wholly misleading to think of religion as the soul of civilization. When we search for firmer reasons to support this conjecture, we find the philosophy of Alfred North Whitehead.

Reflection on the contribution of Christianity and Roman Catholicism to the adventure of ideas which is Western civilization played an integral

[3] The need for religion to deal with the moral fragmentation of modern society has been the theme of the neo-conservative social philosopher Daniel Bell in *The Cultural Contradictions of Capitalism* (New York: Basic Books, 1973) and *The Winding Passage* (New York: Basic Books, 1980). In the political center, sociologist Robert Bellah and his co-authors in *Habits of the Heart: Individualism and Commitment in American Life* (Berkeley: University of California, 1985), William Sullivan in *Reconstructing Public Philosophy* (Berkeley: University of California, 1982) and historian John Patrick Diggins in *The Lost Soul of American Politics* (Berkeley: University of California, 1985) have made similar arguments. More radical is legal philosopher Roberto Mangabeira Unger, *Knowledge and Politics* (New York: Basic Books, 1975), whose professed aim is to reformulate Catholic social theory for the modern age.

part in Whitehead's own view of history and culture. While he fully appreciated the deleterious effects of religious faith for certain developments in European and world history, Whitehead nonetheless contended that religion was the energizing soul of civilization and the strength which brought about major advances in cultural life. "The Adventure of Ideas" is Whitehead's expression for the gradual realization over time of ideals first glimpsed in religious visions of the world.[4]

Whitehead, as a Christian Platonist, believed God is leading humanity through history by setting before it ideals for realization. In this context, he notes the dangers of the sterile repetition of outworn conventions as a mistaken strategy of cultural renewal. There can be, he asserts, no indefinite repetition of any finite ideal. "The pure conservative is fighting against the essence of the universe," he wrote in *Adventure of Ideas*. "Advance or Decay are the only choices to be offered to mankind."[5] As long as experimentation is possible within the limits of a given ideal, Whitehead argued, a society will flourish; but once repetition sets in, then decadence gains a hold. Appreciation gives way to convention; imagination is replaced by sloganeering; the passion for truth is eclipsed by mere cleverness.

"There is an alternative to slow decline," Whitehead wrote. "A race may exhaust a form of civilization without having exhausted its own creative springs of originality. In that case, a quick period of transition may set in, which may or may not be accompanied by dislocations involving widespread unhappiness."[6] Whitehead cited a series of such rapid transformations: the end of the Middle Ages, the Reformation, the late eighteenth century—among others; and he added, "Also let us hope that our present epoch is to be viewed as a period of change to a new civilization, involving in its dislocations a minimum of human misery." In the United States, President Reagan's neoconservative political and economic revolution clearly represents a sharp turn in historical development. Whether it is a change to new ideals with minimal social disruption or a repetition of old ideas leading to increase in human misery is open to question. In the Catholic Church, while there are critics in high places, the period after the Second Vatican Council exemplifies the kind of adaptation to new ideals Whitehead sees as necessary for cultural vitality. The new-found collegiality of the American Bishops in the issuing of their pastoral letters on peace and the economy is a noteworthy example of the seizing of fresh possibilities which is essential to renewal. The efflorescence of *communidades de base* and the rapid spread of

[4] Alfred North Whitehead, *Adventure of Ideas* (New York: Macmillan, 1933), 354.
[5] *Adventure*, 359.
[6] *Ibid.*

liberation theology also represent shifts in the patterns and purposes of church communities from which new life springs. More generally, the emergence of the Third World Church counts as an epochal shift in religious awareness which already has had profound effects on the Church in the United States.

Whitehead was interested in how changes like these come about. Societal renewal, he argued, demanded quick transitions to new ideals, and it is the role of religion to introduce new ideals, to provide the contexts in which they inspire and inform individual and communal character, and to stand behind them as standards of achievement for society and its institutions. On Whitehead's reading at least three things are necessary for social change to transpire happily: (a) a feeling for the contrast between past and future, "between what has been and what may be"; (b) the courage of our hopes, what he calls the nerve for Adventure; and (c) an enspiriting trust in God's power to transform the world, which liberates the deepest springs of committed action—this is the grace Whitehead calls "Peace", the crowning virtue of civilized life.[7]

All three elements, according to Whitehead, are necessary for successful social change. In the contrast of past and future, we discover the projection of ourselves into the future as a fundamental tendency of our lives. Our being, we learn, is not static but tensive; we are stretched between past and future, so that we lean, as it were, into time to come. In addition, the contrast of the actual with the possible is the basis of the cognitive component needed for advance. But Whitehead does not have in mind any bare ideas. He speaks of ideals, dreams, perfections. They are rich in affect and motivational power. They lure and inspire men and women to take on new challenges and to dare new deeds.

In holding to the unity of reason and feeling, as we have already seen, Whitehead shares in one of the recurrent motifs of American religious philosophy. Jonathan Edwards argued the importance of religious affections in relation to orthodox doctrine when he claimed that doctrinal knowledge and speculation without affection never touches the heart of religion.[8] William James celebrated the moral challenge of the future, and John Dewey saw the creative tension between past and future as the key to religious experience. Knowledge and feeling are geared to action.

Of particular importance among the affections is courage. Whitehead speaks of the nerve needed to break with "the safeties of the past" and to meet doubt and opposition head on. Saint Thomas comments of courage that on its positive side it consists of grandeur of vision and

[7] See *Adventure*, chapter 7.

[8] See Jonathan Edwards, *Religious Affections*, ed. John E. Smith (New Haven: Yale University Press, 1959), 120 and 272.

strength of execution.[9] So also, for Whitehead, adventure is boldness of vision combined with the power of realization. Quick transitions to new social arrangements are possible, he wrote, only when "The vigour of the race has . . . rushed forward into the adventure of imagination. The world dreams of things to come," he muses, "and in due season dreams of their realization."[10] But adventure, like courage, has its darker side. New ideas don't always meet with easy acceptance, and grand visions may provoke strenuous opposition. So, adventure may bring with it tragedy. For adventure to succeed, therefore, it requires more than imagination and the lure of novelty. It needs a bedrock of confidence which will be able to withstand failure and disappointment, to meet opposition with determined action, and to overcome resentment with gentle persuasion. Such confidence is found in the gift of peace.

Peace is the assurance which outlasts tragedy and provides a firm trust in the future. The ideals which God sets before us can draw us out of ourselves and make us bold, but nonetheless we can also expect to meet "pain, frustration, loss, tragedy." In the desolation of defeat, peace is the felt conviction that the ideal is not effaced, that its power will still be felt, its perfection enjoyed, and history transformed. Peace, Whitehead wrote, "keeps vivid the sensitiveness to the tragedy as a living agent persuading the world to aim at fineness of achievement beyond the faded level of surrounding fact. Each tragedy is the disclosure of an ideal:— What might have been and was not: What can be."[11] Thus, the divine persuasion inspires us to strain forward "towards the new virtues to make the common life of the City of God what it should be."[12] Thus, the courage to change history is rooted ultimately in God's power to transform us even in our failures.

2. Enculturation as Creative Passage

For Whitehead, then, history is "creative passage" toward new ideals and religion is the factor which brings about change and development in history through the introduction of those new ideals and the inspiring of souls to labor for their realization. "Creative passage" is a theme taken up by Bernard Meland in his theology of culture. Meland, drawing on Whitehead, regards creative passage as "the basic characterization of existence as it applies to all life, to all people, to all cultures." In his essay on Meland, "Appreciative Awareness: The Feeling Dimension in Religious Experience," J. J. Mueller shows how the affective dimension of religious experience leads into unsuspected depths of religious knowl-

---

[9] *Summa theologiae* 2a, IIae, q.128.1.

[10] *Adventure*, 359.

[11] *Adventure*, 369.

[12] *Religion in the Making* (New York: Macmillan, 1926), 39.

edge. According to Mueller, this creative passage takes place not only at the personal level, but at the cultural and institutional level as well, making new depths of awareness possible for increasing numbers of persons.[13] Enculturation is not just a modern-day fad. It is an essential part of the life of faith in society. To be sustained, ideals need to be embodied in institutions, practices, traditions and rules—in the ongoing life of a people.

The authors of this volume are themselves engaged in the work of enculturation. They hope to reinvigorate both church and society by bringing the ideals of the gospel into dialogue with the traditions of this nation. There are two movements in this experiment. The first is the identification of themes and sentiments from within the American tradition which, on the one hand, enjoy strength of appeal within the culture and which, on the other, incline participants in the culture to hear the gospel and come to faith. The second is the work of cultural transformation, the attempt to inspire the culture with the spirit of the gospel.

The first task of an enculturated theology is to identify those themes within the culture which have some resonance with the gospel. In an older terminology, the first requirement is to recognize the *preparatio evangelica*. While some themes of classical American religious philosophy have some parallels in Europe and elsewhere, and while American philosophers were cognizant of European thought and sometimes drew on it, the thinkers (Edwards, Peirce, James, Royce, Whitehead, Hocking, H.R. Niebuhr and Meland) on whom these authors have relied developed philosophies with a distinctly American resonance.

Conversion, for example, though a universal religious phenomenon, has taken on, nonetheless, a very special coloring in the United States from Puritan days, through the Great Awakening, to the evangelical revivals of our own day. In the American tradition, moreover, some notable thinkers, like Edwards and James, have taken up this topic as a major focus of study. Donald Gelpi makes conversion a central element in his treatment of charismatic piety, proposing that social and political conversion must accompany personal religious and affective conversion as it has been known in the Charismatic Movement up to now. For a second case, consider human dignity. Around the world, people acknowledge it in many different ways. But could it be understood as divine reverence, as Hocking and John Stacer suggest, except in a country like ours where respect for others has been a condition of pluralism and liberty? For a third example, take discernment, a topic William Spohn takes up in the light of Edwards's and Niebuhr's theologies. Might this practice have the vast influence it has in contemporary American spir-

---

[13] For Mueller on cultural dimensions of appreciative awareness, see pp. 135–37.

ituality were it not for the orientation of American culture to the future and its practical spirit of enterprise? Thus, these themes, as treated in these essays on and adaptations of American masters, may be expected to serve as avenues of access to the hearts of an American audience, precisely because they tap into special American sensibilities.

The second movement in the process of enculturation is cultural transformation. There are two aspects to the process of enspiriting the secular culture with the gospel. The first is a critical backward look at the culture, identifying its ambiguities and ironies, its problems and failings. At the risk of seeming to divide a single moment of conversion, let me suggest that the critical stage of cultural transformation is the equivalent of the moment of repentance in personal life. It is time for recognizing our social sin and the structures that perpetuate it.

The second phase is the moment of social commitment. To use the parallel of personal conversion again, it is like the sequence of affirming one's faith through the church—the request for baptism (or, in the evangelical tradition, confessing Jesus as Lord and Savior) followed by a life of discipleship. Transformation, as Josiah Royce argued, comes about through a society's dedication to a new center of loyalty and the ideal(s) embodied in that loyalty. That is a position shared by Richard Niebuhr and expounded here by Frank Oppenheim.[14]

In the history of the Christian Church, for example, Whitehead saw the Church's commitment to Jesus Christ embodied in a succession of ideals which gave focus to the energies of the Western world: the dignity of the person, the unity of the human community, liberty of conscience, the equality of persons, and so on. No doubt, were he to survey the situation today, he would see the Church as a leaven in new ways: as a defender of the poor and the oppressed, as a living symbol of the unity of humankind in a divided world, as an upholder of the rights of individuals and communities in the face of economic exploitation and political regression.

Christianity, Whitehead wrote, has "constituted an unrivalled program for reform . . . The progress of humanity can be defined as the process of transforming society so as to make the original Christian ideals more practicable . . . "[15] "Progress," he wrote, "consists in modifying the laws of nature so that the Republic on Earth may conform to that Society to be discerned ideally by the divination of Wisdom."[16] In sum, transformation involves taking on new goals which are fitted to the exigencies of

---

[14] See Royce, *Philosophy of Loyalty* (New York, 1908), H.R. Niebuhr, *The Responsible Self*, and Oppenheim, pp. 95–117.

[15] *Adventure*, 18.   [16] *Adventure*, 53.

the age, both in meeting its problems and in attaining its historic possibilities.

Classic American philosophy assists in the work of transformation under both these aspects. It addresses the deficiencies of the culture of the United States and it also points up novel ideals for future realization. Among the deficiencies of American culture addressed by the nation's classic authors are: the superficial practicality and economic rationality of a business culture which manifests itself in a lack of contemplative awareness and sensitivity; a radical individualism which neglects the solidarity of men and women in creation and redemption; and a vaunting nationalism which tempts the sovereignty of God. To each of these faults, our authors offer a remedy. For superficial pragmatism and utilitarianism, they prescribe "appreciative awareness" (Mueller) and "a grammar of affections" (Spohn); as an antidote to the alienation produced by radical individualism, they recommend reverence (Stacer) and social and political conversion (Gelpi); and as a cure for nationalism, they propose love of the Great Community (Oppenheim).

3. Creative Passage in the Life of Faith

A society's creative passage through history consists in the gradual realization over time of new ideals. The themes of conversion and discernment treated in the essays by Gelpi and Spohn, and Mueller's presentation of appreciative awareness represent dimensions of religious experience in which such creative advance can take place. They are the processes in which new ideals arise, develop, mature, and subsequently enter into the life of the larger community to re-shape and transform it. The affective conversion represented, for example, by the charismatic renewal can be seen as a religious happening, as Gelpi understands it, with critical implications for legalism and formalism in the Church's liturgical piety.[17] It can also be taken to be a critique of "the abstract society" in which we live. Similarly, Gelpi's proposal that charismatic piety ought to lead the members of the renewal to social responsibility and political action is an indictment of a society in which the affective life has been too long severed from the domains of reason and action. In calling for the kind of political conversion among Catholic charismatics which has taken place already among socially conscious evangelicals, like the Sojourners' Community, Gelpi is contributing to that "program of discontent" whereby Christianity transforms our inherited culture.

[17] For Gelpi's interpretation of the criticism of liturgical piety inherent in the charismatic renewal, see pp. 35–40.

If conversion is the beginning of the Spirit's stirring of the waters, the work of re-creation continues and is deepened in the process of discernment. For the Spirit is known not only in the conversion experience, but also in the endeavor of learning and doing God's will. The Spirit is the lure to novel ways of living the gospel as well as a spur to repentance. Accordingly, responsibility to God involves openness and creativity, so that the new tasks to which humanity is invited may be appropriated and realized.

H. R. Niebuhr, much like Whitehead, saw that when we respond to the actions of others upon us in the world, the one to whom we respond is ultimately God's own self. Discovering "the fitting response" to the problems and possibilities of our society and our moment in history demands that we respond to God's action upon us, that we allow ourselves to be affected by the divine Beauty. Accordingly, discernment is more than a private act of personal piety and individual devotion; it is a matter of discovering what God is doing in society and history and aligning ourselves with the divine initiative.[18] In Whitehead's terminology, this is the process of setting before ourselves the ideals by which God renews the world.

Ideals cannot be discerned, however, in the abstract. We cannot identify them merely, as it were, by surveying the landscape. It is not a matter of scanning the facts and deciding by some leap of the emotion what we shall do. Rather, discernment consists in expanding one's character, in broadening and deepening one's sensibilities in receptivity to the gospel message and God's present action upon us. As Whitehead wrote in *Religion in the Making*, "Your character is developed according to your faith. This is the primary religious truth from which no one can escape. Religion is the force of belief cleansing the inward parts."[19]

Thus, William Spohn, building on Edwards and Niebuhr, emphasizes the role of the religious affections in discernment. Discernment is deeper than choice. It is affective attunement. To learn God's will, or in Whitehead's terminology, to discern the divine ideals, it is necessary to let one's deepest tendencies be transmuted by meditation on the gospel and to allow one's personality to be refigured in the image of Christ. In other words, discernment involves contemplation of and growing attachment to the person of Christ.[20]

Of course, one does not conform oneself to the image of Christ by an act of the will, but rather by opening up deeper and deeper layers of one's heart in response to the person of Christ. That is to say, growth comes

[18] See H. R. Niebuhr, *The Responsible Self*, 126, and *The Meaning of Revelation* (New York: Macmillan, 1960), 64; also Spohn, pp. 49–73.

[19] *Religion in the Making*, 15.

[20] See Spohn, pp. 58–62.

from contemplation. This activity itself is more like attentive receptivity than a deliberate act of "unselfing." One is drawn, not just with greater force, but with increasing sensitivity, by God's beauty unveiled in the person of Christ.

The importance of Meland's notion of "appreciative awareness," as presented by J. J. Mueller, is to restate for us the profound truth that religious knowledge consists in the elevation of consciousness through a unity with God in which ego is effaced or, better, transformed. Analogies may be found in the contemplation of a great work of art or of mountain vastness, but they are weak comparisons. "Appreciative awareness" gives rise to the energy of creative passage as there is an increase in sensitivity to God's beauty drawing us out of our self-concern to a wider, deeper life, rich in relationships.[21] Writing of the key religious experience of peace, Whitehead says something quite similar. Peace, he writes:

> is the removal of inhibition and not its introduction. It results in a wider sweep of conscious interest. It enlarges the field of attention. Thus Peace is self-control at its widest,—at the width where 'self' has been lost, and interest has been transferred to coordinations wider than personality.[22]

Thus, "appreciative awareness" is not just a stance of contemplative receptivity. It is an active state. It is part of the transformation of character in alignment with the persuasive power of divine Beauty.

The union of affectivity (and thought) with action found in the conversion/discernment process, as we have seen, is characteristic of the tradition of American religious philosophy. Affectivity, thought and action are elements in a living whole. Logic, morality, art and religion, Whitehead claimed in *Modes of Thought*, are all species of "Importance," that aspect of feeling whereby perspective is imposed on the universe of things felt. They are all ways of "grading the effectiveness of things about us in proportion to their interest."[23]

Perhaps the holism of the American religious philosophy is best captured in Whitehead's oxymoron "the efficacy of Beauty." Again, writing of Peace, he says, it is:

> primarily a trust in the efficacy of Beauty. It is a sense that fineness of achievement is as it were a key to unlocking treasures that the narrow nature of things would keep remote. . . . The trust in the self-justification of Beauty introduces faith, where reason fails to reveal the details.[24]

Thus, an aesthetic experience provides the ultimate grounds for action.

[21] See Muller, pp. 121–43.

[22] *Adventure*, 367.

[23] *Modes of Thought* (New York: Macmillan/Free Press, 1966), 11.

[24] *Adventure of Ideas*, 367.

The mode of perception is aesthetic, but the manner of attainment includes the full scope of historic action. At the same time, in the moment of religious insight Whitehead also acknowledges that reason has reached a limit, but he nonetheless assumes a compatibility between rationality and Beauty's divine persuasion.

Discernment, as I have pointed out, takes place in a reading of the religious affections. Peace is one of those affections. In their articles, John Stacer and Frank Oppenheim discuss two others, namely, reverence and love.

Plato in *The Laws* took the reemergence of reverence to be the signal which marked every cultural renewal, just as its diminishment signalled impending decline.[25] In much the same way, Whitehead comments, "the growth of reverence" is "the foundation of respect of man for man." Without reverence, he believed, "society lapses into riot."[26] In proposing a theology of reverence as part of the renewal of American religious thinking, therefore, John Stacer had solid precedent. In the affection of reverence we may well have an antidote to the violence and rapacity of American society today.

Among moral philosophers there is a current of thought which argues that liberal political philosophy can no longer suffice as a source of moral norms for contemporary society.[27] In his Gifford Lectures, for example, Basil Mitchell has proposed that only a return to Christian theological sources can provide the framework of belief needed to uphold the deepest values of our culture. Respect for persons, the cardinal value of modern society, he contends, cannot be sustained apart from faith in God's love for humankind and the destiny of communion with God which is the completion of that love.[28] Stacer urges his readers to consider God's presence, cherishing and persuading as manifestations of God's reverence for human beings. Our reverence for one another is, as it were, a participation in the divine reverence. This novel argument lends support to the concept of human dgnity which has played such a key role in the Catholic Church's defense of human rights. Reverence, understood as dispositions of presence, cherishing and persuading, helps one interpret how we are to respond to others in keeping with their inestimable worth.

One of the directions to which Stacer points in drawing out the implications of divine reverence is toward global justice. Frank Oppen-

[25] See *The Laws*, Translated with Notes and Interpretative Essay by Thomas L. Pangle (New York: Basic Books, 1980), Book III.

[26] *Adventure of Ideas*, 126.

[27] The best known argument of this sort is Alisdair MacIntyre's *After Virtue* (Notre Dame: University of Notre Dame, 1981); I find Basil Mitchell's reasoning in *Morality: Religious and Secular* (Oxford: Clarendon Press, 1980) more persuasive.

[28] *Morality: Religious and Secular*, 122–137.

heim in his piece points in the same direction, but offers still another way to the ideals God sets before us. Certainly, one of the more serious impediments to global justice is nationalism. The call of Pope John XXIII more than twenty years ago that nations must act on behalf of the universal common good has been forgotten in a succession of trials and spasms of jingoism. Oppenheim tries to address the excesses of nationalism and the ideal of global community through Josiah Royce's conception of love for "the Great Community."[29]

The Great Community provides a vehicle for imagining our national destiny in the context of a world community. Royce's concept has many affinities with Catholic social theology. I have already noted the parallel with the universal common good as described by John XXIII. But generally, Catholic social theology sees human beings as communal and social. Human identity is had in wider and wider circles of relationship. Recent Church teaching, for example, sees this reality manifest in the growth of socialization within societal institutions. Moreover, Catholic faith affirms that this movement takes place in the world as well as in the Church. In both, Christian love (charity) grows in its power until it reaches fulfillment in the Kingdom of God. In a similar way, the Great Community and the Beloved Community stand in relationship to one another. Love is the force at work in both—in one partially; in the other fully, as it will be in the Church at the end of history. Thus, Oppenheim suggests our narrow patriotism may be transformed into a loyalty to the human family through the affection of a personal, wholehearted, practical love for every human self and for that Great Community since only by commitment to it can the life of any human self become ultimately meaningful.

FAITH'S ADVENTURE: RELIGIOUS ACTUALISM

I have argued that the affective and contemplative dimensions of the classic American religious philosophies and theologies are responses to the superficiality of the activist American temper. At the same time, I have asserted that the religious affections, discernment, conversion, and so on, are part of an overall pragmatist method. Classic American philosophy is interested in the outcomes of religious beliefs, affections and experiences. The psychoanalyst Erik Erikson may capture the spirit of the pragmatism of American religious philosophy when he writes of "religious actualism." By this he means that religious truth, in Jonathan Edwards's vital sense of that term and in Cardinal Newman's sense of "real knowledge," is revealed in action.

Erikson's phrase derives from his study of Gandhi's "experiments with

---

[29] See Oppenheim, pp. 97–117.

truth." These were acts of religious discipline and militant nonviolence through which Gandhi sought to win justice and independence for the people of India.[30] The experiment means that justice does not exist in the abstract, but in what emerges when people confront one another in a search for a common expression of respect for human dignity. Gandhi tried in many ways to achieve this respect for his people. His campaigns and even his personal efforts at self-control were his experiments. It seems to me that the pragmatism of American religious philosophy needs to be interpreted in a similar way. It looks for the outcomes of belief and states of religious awareness. It is pragmatic in that it is disposed to experiment to find different ways in which the truth of faith can be incarnated. It must experiment for there are new embodiments of the divine ideals still to be found. It is unafraid of novelty, because it is lured on by the divine ideals of peace, reverence and love.

The examples of this kind of experimentation in the life of the Church today are numerous. William Spohn suggests that the martyrdom/exile shift, a dramatic alteration in Israel's identity as God's people, might be applied to the United States today as a way of responding to the demand for nuclear disarmament. He thus takes an experiment from biblical times and suggests its pertinence to the present political situation.[31] But the United States has also had other experiments with truth, including the abolitionist movement and more recently the civil rights movement. John XXIII, Vatican II and subsequent Church teaching provide a Catholic analog to experiments with truth in the reading of the signs of the times. Reading the signs of the times is a way of assessing the *sensus fidelium* and the *consensus gentium* with respect to how God is calling us to realize new ideals as part of humanity's adventure through history. Thus, the American Bishops' reflection on nuclear war and more recently their draft pastoral on the economy are also part of that program of discontent, as Whitehead called it, through which society is renewed by its receptivity to the divine persuasion. They are in keeping with the pragmatic spirit of American religious philosophy's experiments with truth.

CONCLUSION

In the forms of Catholic theology, locating a sharp dividing line between faith and culture is more difficult than we sometimes imagine. Whether we are dealing with patristic, scholastic, transcendental Thomist or liberation theologies, faith and culture interpenetrate. Living the life of faith, moreover, it is even more difficult to conceive of a cleft between

---

[30] Erik Erikson, *Gandhi's Truth* (New York: Norton, 1969), 396.
[31] See Spohn, pp. 65–66.

what we believe and the way we live. If belief shapes character, as Whitehead, and several of our authors (Spohn, Gelpi, and Mueller in particular) contend, then belief will also affect our societal and cultural forms. Apart from a lived relationship with God which widens our hearts and steels our commitments, alterations in our institutions lack significance. And equally, faith without the power to inspire and transform our institutions lacks life and motion. Faith and culture belong together. The adventure of ideas is a way of describing their joint movement through history.

Our authors provide perspectives on the ways in which faith is an energizing force in history. Conversion is one phase of the creative passage in which people are re-oriented so that the divine persuasion can lead us to perceive new ideals. Discernment is the process of aligning oneself with God's activity through growth in those religious affections which conform one to Christ through appreciative awareness. Finally, in reverence for persons and love of the Great Community we have two affections and ideals which the world and the people of the United States very much need today to meet the challenges of global peace and justice. American religious philosophy in focusing religious experience for us as interior growth and outward movement serves the adventure of ideas by making us conscious of how our own lives and that of our society can be renewed by yielding to the divine persuasion.

Donald L. Gelpi

Conversion: The Challenge of Contemporary Charismatic Piety

Donald L. Gelpi, S.J., is professor of historical/systematic theology in the Jesuit School of Theology at Berkeley and a member of the Graduate Theological Union faculty. He has engaged himself prominently in the theology of Karl Rahner, religious life and the vows, sacramental theology, pneumatology, and the charismatic renewal. He is the author of, among other books, *Experiencing God: A Theology of Human Emergence*, and *The Divine Mother: A Trinitarian Theology of the Holy Spirit*.

F EW MOVEMENTS have shaped popular religious attitudes in the United States more profoundly than revivalism. Between 1739 and 1742 new-light evangelical preachers crisscrossed the thirteen English colonies summoning their citizens to a shared experience of religious conversion and renewal that they described as a Great Awakening. The revival stirred millenarian hopes in the twice-born that through the very experience of religious renewal a predestining God was preparing America for an era of unparalleled peace and prosperity. The revival appealed to members of all the established churches and ignored colonial boundaries as well. It left the citizens of thirteen independent colonies not only with a new ecumenical awareness of Christian solidarity but also with a nascent sense of national identity.[1]

In 1801 the Second Great Awakening erupted at Cane Ridge, Kentucky, but soon swept the coastal cities as well. It was followed by wave upon wave of revivalistic fervor. Always a source of controversy, evangelical revivalism forced Christians of all denominations to grapple with the role and function of religion in the United States.[2] Revivalistic cultivation of affective fervor also fed the American romantic impulse by helping to inspire the transcendental search for an intuitive experience of God.[3]

[1] Alan Heimert and Perry Miller, eds., *The Great Awakening* (Indianapolis: Bobbs Merrill, 1967); Alan Heimert, *Religion and the American Mind: From the Great Awakening to the Revolution* (Cambridge: Harvard, 1966); C. C. Goen, "Jonathan Edwards: A New Departure in Eschatology," *Church History* 28 (1959) 25-40.

[2] Perry Miller, *The Life of the Mind in America* (New York: Harcourt, Brace, World, 1965).

[3] In 1831 Charles Grandison Finney brought the Second Great Awakening to Boston. Shortly before resigning his Unitarian pulpit, Ralph Waldo Emerson preached to his staid Unitarian congregation on revivalism, eulogizing the principles on which the movement rests. He found fault only with the irrational character of the emotionalism it generated. His reflections can be found in his unpublished manuscripts in the Houghton Library at Harvard: "Sermons," H (111 A) 7-10, H (111 B) 1-11. When Emerson abandoned his pulpit to become a circuit lecturer, he seems to have ambitioned a genteel religious revival that

25

Both spiritualism and Mormonism emerged from upstate New York, a region so frequently evangelized it was dubbed the "burnt-over district." And indeed both movements could scarcely be conceived apart from a society suffused with revivalistic fervor.[4] Nor could that distinctly American blend of faith healing and rational enlightenment known as Christian Science.[5] Moreover, as the nation lurched toward civil conflict, the moral soul-searching inculcated by evangelical piety seems in the case of many to have lent popular religious sanction to the abolitionist crusade.

Immigrant American Catholicism in its embattled confrontation with waspish nativism and Know-Nothingism held itself aloof from evangelical revivalism during the nineteenth century. But the Catholic community practiced its own form of revivalistic piety. Itinerant clerical evangelists preached parish missions and measured their success by the Catholic equivalent of an altar call: the lines of penitents that crowded to the confessional testified to the power of the missionary's evangelizing rhetoric.[6]

Led by saints like Francis of Assisi, Dominic, Ignatius Loyola, and others, Catholics have known repeated "revivals" of piety. But in the latter half of the twentieth century the American Catholic Church paradoxically found itself in the forefront of a religious revival in the evangelical mode that quickly spread to the other mainline churches in America and then expanded to international proportions. Because the revival fused elements of traditional Roman Catholic and Pentecostal piety, its leaders first described themselves as "Catholic Pentecostals."[7] But at the behest of the American episcopacy, who felt chary about the denominational connotations of the term "pentecostals," the revival was renamed "the Catholic charismatic renewal." When the new name was initially suggested, it seemed innocent enough; but it has, as we shall see, bred a certain amount of pastoral and theological confusion.

Like any popular devotion, the charismatic renewal boasts its glories even while it labors under a certain number of miseries.[8] A predominantly

avoided the limitations of the Second Great Awakening by inspiring a religiously motivated cultural revival.

[4] Slater Brown, *The Heyday of Spiritualism* (New York: Pocketbook, 1972); Fawn M. Brodie, *No Man Knows My History* (New York; Knopf, 1945).

[5] Julius Silberger, Jr., "Mary Baker Eddy," *American Heritage* 32 (Dec. 1980) 56–64.

[6] Jay P. Dolan, *Catholic Revivalism: The American Experience* (Notre Dame: Univ. of Notre Dame, 1978).

[7] Kevin and Dorothy Ranaghan, *Catholic Pentecostals* (New York: Paulist, 1969); Edward D. O'Connor, *The Pentecostal Movement in the Catholic Church* (Notre Dame: Ave Maria, 1971).

[8] For a description of the charismatic movement, see Richard Quebedaux, *The New Charismatics* (New York: Doubleday, 1976).

lay-led movement, it has brought thousands of Christians to an experience of personal conversion and giftedness. It has not only restored the Bible to participating Catholics but transformed it into a living word. A potentially powerful form of grass-roots ecumenism, the charismatic renewal has instilled in the hearts of many otherwise ecumenically apathetic Christians of different denominations a longing for sacramental communion with one another. By inspiring practical faith in the Spirit's anointing, shared charismatic prayer has transformed abstract Catholic belief that the Holy Spirit animates the Church into a lived experience of the Spirit's presence. Charismatic Christians who bring to liturgical worship the habit of active participation in shared, spontaneous, charismatic prayer suffuse traditional sacramental cult with fervent personal and communal piety. And from their reading of Scripture, they have spontaneously reappropriated the theologically correct habit of ascribing all graced enlightenment to the Holy Spirit.[9]

One might easily expand this list of charismatic virtues. But popular charismatic piety also suffers all too often from a certain amount of human frailty and folly. Its miseries reflect the limitations of the two Christian traditions the movement blends. Charismatic Christians learned from Protestant Pentecostals to love the Bible as a living word, but too often they also learned to read Scripture fundamentalistically. And in their efforts to shore up Christian family life or to order large, unwieldy prayer groups or covenant communities, Catholic charismatics

---

[9] Donald L. Gelpi, S.J., *Charism and Sacrament: A Theology of Christian Conversion* (New York: Paulist, 1976). The term "spirit" has been all but co-opted by philosophy. As a philosophical term, "spirit" signifies "immaterial." In transcendental philosophy it connotes the horizon of the spiritual powers of intellect and will. But in both the Old and New Testaments "the Holy Spirit" signifies the divine "breathing," a divine, gracious, life-giving principle of empowering illumination. In the present article we use the terms "Spirit" and "Holy Spirit" in their biblical sense. Contemporary Trinitarian theologians stand divided on the advisability of speaking of Father, Son, and Spirit as divine persons. Karl Rahner, following Karl Barth, advocates calling them "modes" rather than persons. Heribert Mühlen and Jürgen Moltmann defend the term "person." The debate remains unresolved because, as far as I can judge, none of these theologians offers a clear principle of verification which would allow us to judge between the truth or adequacy of conflicting Trinitarian constructs. The missions of the divine persons provide such a principle. Apart from the historical missions of the Son and of the Spirit, we have no information about how the divine persons relate to one another. Jesus' "Abba experience" is now conceded as historical by all questers for the historical Jesus. It can only be described as interpersonal. It was inspired in Jesus by the Holy Spirit. The Spirit's distinction from the Son is historically revealed in the distinction of Their missions. As a distinct source of interpersonal consciousness within the Godhead, the Spirit cannot be less than a divine person, even though the term "person" can be applied only analogously to humans and to the members of the divine triad. I discussed these and other related questions in more detail in my work *The Divine Mother: A Trinitarian Theology of the Holy Spirit.*

have sometimes involved the authoritarianism and sexism that mar the Roman tradition.[10]

In so speaking, I no way wish to stereotype all the participants in the charismatic renewal as fundamentalistic, authoritarian, and sexist. Nor do I suggest that they have cornered the market on these three neurotic religious aberrations. All three flourish in the right wing of the Catholic Church.

Moreover, some of the blame for the aberrations in charismatic communities must be laid at the doorstep of the institutional Church. The Catholic episcopacy's early concern to provide pastoral guidelines for the charismatic renewal has matured into a general acceptance of the movement as a legitimate expression of contemporary Catholic piety. Most dioceses in this country now boast a director or official liaison for charismatic Catholics, and these diocesan directors meet annually in a national convention to give sound pastoral guidelines to the renewal. Nonetheless, significant numbers of the diocesan clergy still greet the charismatic movement with coolness or benign neglect. Such negative attitudes have helped preserve the predominantly lay character of the movement's leadership, but they have also marginalized more than one charismatic group or foolishly and needlessly forced it into an adversary stance with respect to ecclesiastical structures.

Nor can the Catholic theological community avoid shouldering some of the responsibility for aberrations within the charismatic renewal. Although a handful of theologians have associated themselves with the movement and have attempted to provide it with sound catechesis, most of the American Catholic theological community have for a variety of reasons failed to respond in any visible way to the pastoral needs of charismatic Christians or to reflect on the revelatory and ecumenical significance of this spontaneous, grass-roots transformation of lay Catholic spirituality.

In point of fact, the Roman Catholic tradition offers many neglected theological resources for reflecting on a charismatic Christian experience. Since the early part of the nineteenth century, the Catholic theological community, troubled by the fact that in the Roman Catholic Church the Holy Spirit had been transformed into "the forgotten God," began a plodding academic retrieval of biblical and systematic pneumatology. Early efforts bore fruit in Leo XIII's encyclical *Divinum illud munus* (1897). The Pope's letter summarized and systematized the salient points of a medieval theology of the Spirit, but its abstract scholastic language

---

[10] Joseph H. Fichter, S.J., *The Catholic Cult of the Paraclete* (New York: Sheed and Ward, 1975) 39–57; Josephine Ford, *Which Way for Catholic Pentecostals?* (New York: Harper and Row, 1976).

sparked little living devotion in most of the faithful. The document, however, called attention to the Spirit's charismatic activity, and a second wave of pneumatological research bore fruit in Pope Pius XII's *Mystici corporis* (1943). The new encyclical proclaimed that the Holy Spirit animates the body of Christ as its living soul and described the charisms of the Spirit as a perennial endowment of the Church. By the time the Second Vatican Council was convoked, theologians had reached a solid consensus that the charisms of the Spirit provide a correct theological rubric for understanding lay spirituality. In the course of the debates at Vatican II, the bishops scrapped the authoritarian, hierarchical schema on the Church originally prepared by conservative Vatican theologians and voted initial approval to a revised schema that underscored heavily the charismatic character of lay spirituality. Having affirmed a charismatic laity, the bishops decided, somewhat tardily, that they also needed to assert the charismatic character of ordained ministry as well. As a consequence, one finds in the documents of Vatican II a somewhat artificial distinction between hierarchical charisms and charismatic charisms.[11] Subsequent to Vatican II, some theologians have suggested that the charismatic action of the Spirit supplies the ultimate principle of order within the Church, a principle more fundamental than laws, traditions, rules, and regulations.[12]

But besides fostering a lively interest in the charisms of the Spirit, popular charismatic piety often adopts religious attitudes and practices traditionally inculcated by evangelical revivalism: a conversion experience that establishes an affective relationship with the person of Jesus; public personal testimony to the action of the Spirit in one's own life; an evangelizing rhetoric that addresses the heart; a piety focused on feeling; faith healing; shared spontaneous prayer.

Evangelical revivalism has shaped popular religious attitudes in this country so profoundly that the participation of the American Catholic Church in a revival in the evangelical mode stands as an important landmark in the indigenization of American Catholicism. Through the charismatic renewal, the American Catholic community has in effect joined the revivalistic mainstream of popular evangelical religion. Moreover, in a land in which revivalism offers a fairly permanent way of life, the Catholic Church can anticipate the very real possibility of waves of revivalistic fervor among its members. We Catholics would do well, then, to come to theological and pastoral terms with the implications of

---

[11] *Lumen gentium* 4.

[12] Gotthold Hasenhüttl, *Charisma: Ordnungsprinzip der Kirche* (Freiburg: Herder, 1967); Gabriel Murphy, *Charisms and Church Renewal* (Rome: Catholic Book Agency, 1965); Hans Küng, *The Church* (New York: Herder, 1967) 150–202.

movements like the charismatic renewal more systematically than we have done heretofore.

In the present chapter I will attempt to probe some of the theological and pastoral implications of popular charismatic piety. Charismatic piety, like revivalistic, summons one to conversion. In section 1 I will explore some important dynamics of Christian conversion. In section 2 I will reflect on some of the ways in which the construct of conversion elaborated in section 1 allows us to come to terms with some of the inauthenticities present in both Catholic and evangelical piety. I will also begin to reflect on the ways in which the authentic elements in both these traditions can mutually reinforce one another, especially through the charismatic transformation of sacramental worship. In section 3 I will begin to probe the experience of charismatically transformed sacramental worship for the light it throws on an authentic Christian conversion. Section 4 continues reflection on the theological implications of the blending of charismatic and sacramental forms of prayer. In it I argue for the charismatic unity of the sacramental system and for the charismatic nature of sacramental experience. In section 5 I will reflect briefly on the ecumenical dimensions of shared charismatic prayer and on its potential to effect social change.

I

Classical Protestant Pentecostalism emerged from a revivalistic impulse in the Methodist church called the Holiness Movement. It resulted more immediately from the ministry of Charles Fox Parham and William J. Seymour. Parham began his career as a lay preacher in the Congregational Church. But after experiencing a temporary loss of faith and then a reconversion to God, Parham was ordained a Methodist minister. He believed church membership helpful but did not require it of those to whom he preached. He sought rather to evoke from them a radical break with sin that resulted from a violent internal struggle. He believed that sanctification could begin only after sin had been eradicated from the heart. He preached the healing power of faith and that the Holy Spirit visibly transforms the sanctified.

In 1898 he founded the Bethel Healing Home in Topeka, Kansas, later to become the Bethel Bible College. Study of Acts 2 convinced some of Parham's parishioners that the gift of tongues provides conclusive evidence of Spirit baptism. When Parham prayed over one of them, a Miss Ozman, she began suddenly and disconcertingly speaking in tongues. Soon thereafter other members of the congregation also received the gift. One of Parham's disciples, William Seymour, carried the Pentecostal message to the west coast. He preached the Azuza Street revival in Los

Angeles. He proclaimed his message by and large to the poor and to the uneducated and brought them to an experience of conversion and Spirit baptism.[13]

The experience of the first Pentecostals gave rise to a theoretical construct for understanding the process of conversion. Prior to receiving the gift of tongues, the first Pentecostals had been practicing Christians. They had in effect experienced a religious conversion. But until they had received the gift of tongues, they did not regard themselves as Spirit-baptized. Moreover, they found that Spirit baptism only inaugurated a process of ongoing transformation in faith. They conceived of graced transformation, therefore, as a three-stage process: conversion, then Spirit baptism whose visible sign was glossolalia, finally sanctification.[14]

From the standpoint of a traditional Roman Catholic theology of grace, such a construct of conversion leaves something to be desired. Catholic sacramental theology associates Spirit baptism with the rite of initiation, although, as Vatican II teaches, that rite only inaugurates a process of lifelong transformation in the Spirit. Traditional Catholic theology also looks upon the infusion of the theological virtues and of the gifts (*dona*) of the Holy Spirit as sanctifying, and it refuses to point to any single charism (*gratia gratis data*) like tongues as certification of Spirit baptism, although, as we shall see, a sound Roman Catholic theology of conversion ought to make room for a pentecostal moment within the process of ongoing conversion.[15]

But anyone who criticizes a particular theological position as inadequate ought by all rights to suggest a more viable alternative. The work of Bernard Lonergan points the way toward a subtler and more adequate construct of conversion than that proposed by classical Pentecostalism.[16]

[13] John A. Hardon, *The Protestant Churches of America* (New York: Image, 1969) 169–83.

[14] Walter Hollenweger, *The Pentecostals: The Charismatic Movement in the Churches* (Minneapolis: Augsburg, 1972); Frederick Dale Brunner, *A Theology of the Holy Spirit* (London: Hodder and Stoughton, 1971); James Dunn, *Baptism in the Holy Spirit* (Naperville: Allenson, 1970).

[15] Gelpi, *Charism and Sacrament* passim.

[16] Bernard Lonergan, S.J., *Method in Theology* (New York: Herder and Herder, 1972). See also William James, *The Varieties of Religious Experience* (New York: Longmans, 1907); E. T. Clark, *The Psychology of Religious Awakening* (New York; Macmillan, 1929); J. Geweiss, "Metanoia in Neuen Testament," *Die Kirche in der Welt* 1 (1948) 2, 149 ff.; Gordon W. Allport, *The Individual and His Religion* (New York: Macmillan, 1950); Arthur Darby Nock, *Conversion: The Old and the New in Religion from Alexander the Great to Augustine of Hippo* (New York: Oxford, 1952); Romano Guardini, *The Conversion of St. Augustine* (Westminster, Md.: Newman, 1960); Bernard Haring, *The Law of Christ* 1 (Westminster, Md.: Newman, 1961) 387–481; Walter E. Conn, *Conversion: Perspectives on Personal and Social Transformation* (New York: Alba, 1978); Gelpi, *Charism and Sacrament*; idem, *Experiencing God: A Theology of Human Emergence* (New York: Paulist, 1981).

In his original construct of conversion, Lonergan distinguished three moments in the conversion process: religious, intellectual, and moral. He has since conceded the need to add a fourth: psychic or affective conversion.[17]

Lonergan himself describes conversion as a decision that creates a horizon.[18] I myself prefer, for a variety of reasons, to avoid the language of horizon.[19] Let us, then, define a conversion in a preliminary fashion as a decision that creates a strictly normative frame of reference.

Frames of reference provide contexts for responding evaluatively to oneself or one's world. We should distinguish strictly normative frames of reference from explanatory ones. An explanatory frame of reference provides a context for understanding things other than one's own personally responsible choices. It enjoys a normative character to this extent: in explanatory frames of reference one seeks to predict the way in which persons or things in one's total environment ought to be expected to behave. But in a strictly normative frame of reference one measures the motives and consequences of one's own personal decisions against ideals personally acknowledged as emotionally, intellectually, morally, and religiously binding. Conversion, then, creates a strictly normative frame of reference, because in conversion one decides to take personal responsibility for one's subsequent development in some area of one's experience. Such a decision constitutes a conversion from irresponsible to responsible behavior, i.e., to behavior which incarnates in concrete situations the ideals to which the convert stands personally committed.

The laws that govern human affectivity differ from the laws of speculative thought. Both differ from the laws that govern moral deliberation. And all three can function independently of religious faith. One may, then, distinguish four different realms of experience for whose subsequent

---

[17] Robert M. Doran, *Subject and Psyche* (Washington, D.C.: University Press of America, 1977); Gelpi, *Charism and Sacrament* and *Experiencing God*; Bernard Lonergan, S.J., "Reality, Myth, Symbol," in Alan M. Olsen, ed., *Myth, Symbol, and Reality* (Notre Dame: Univ. of Notre Dame, 1980) 31–37.

[18] Lonergan, *Method in Theology* 131–32.

[19] The term "horizon" is commonly used in existential circles, where the horizon of cognition is contrasted with the individual persons and things that lie within the horizon. The horizon of the mind cannot be grasped as such, since it is often supposed to enjoy virtual infinity. But things within the horizon of cognition can be known as such, for they remain both finite and intelligible. Existential theologians commonly equate the virtually infinite horizon of the mind with God. Paul Tillich has grasped quite clearly the implications of such an equation. If God is the horizon of human aspiration, the divine reality cannot be grasped as such, cannot be revealed as such within space and time. The incarnation of a divine person then becomes inconceivable, as does a tripersonal God. These conclusions suggest that the philosophical term "horizon" can, in its implications, lead to conclusions irreconcilable with divine revelation. Cf. Paul Tillich, *Systematic Theology* (Chicago: Univ. of Chicago, 1967).

development one may independently assume converted, personal responsibility: affective, speculative, moral, and religious. The realm of affectivity includes sensory images (which enjoy emotional coloring); imageless feelings like sympathy, love, anger, fear, or guilt; remembered images; and the rich polymorphic life of the intuitive imagination. The realm of speculation encompasses every human attempt to provide a controlled, rationally consistent, inferential account of reality. Experience takes on a moral character when it is judged in the light of realities and values that make absolute and ultimate ethical claims. We affirm the moral ultimacy of a reality or value when we are willing not only to live but to die for it; we affirm its moral absoluteness when we uphold its ultimacy in every circumstance. Finally, experience takes on a religious character when we assent in faith to some historical, revelatory self-communication of God.

Besides identifying frames of reference within conversion, one may also speak of three important dynamics within the total process of Christian conversion: (1) religious conversion mediates between affective and moral conversion; (2) intellectual conversion seeks to inform affective, religious, and moral conversion; (3) religious conversion transvalues in faith affective, intellectual, and moral conversion. Let us reflect on each of these dynamics in turn.

In his *Treatise concerning Religious Affections* Jonathan Edwards identified the first dynamic. He conceived the process of conversion as a repentant confrontation with one's own sinfulness that frees the heart to consent to the divine beauty incarnate in Jesus and in Jesus-like people. Christian practice, or the willingness to live by the moral demands of the gospel, tests the authenticity of that consent of faith.[20] William James and C. S. Peirce offer secularized though convergent accounts of this dynamic within the conversion process. Religious repentance causes us to face the repressed anger, fear, and guilt that separate us from God and other persons. As those negative feelings are healed, the heart's capacity to respond to the divine beauty incarnate in Jesus and Jesus-like people expands. That same divine beauty motivates assent to Jesus as the definitive historical self-revelation of God. Consent to that divine act of self-revelation demands that the convert live a life which incarnates the values and ideals Jesus himself lived and proclaimed. In other words, in an integral experience of Christian conversion religious conversion mediates between affective and moral conversion.

The philosophy of C. S. Peirce suggests a second dynamic within

[20] Jonathan Edwards, *A Treatise concerning Religious Affections*, ed. John E. Smith (New York: Yale, 1959); *The Nature of True Virtue*, ed. William K. Frankena (Ann Arbor: Univ. of Michigan, 1969); Roland Delattre, *Beauty and Sensibility in the Thought of Jonathan Edwards* (New Haven: Yale Univ., 1968).

conversion: intellectual conversion ought to inform the other three kinds. Peirce, like Edwards, believed that the spontaneous attractiveness of divine beauty motivates initial religious assent. He also believed that every human being ought in addition to seek to understand how to cultivate habits of emotional growth that foster and sustain such consent. He called the quest for such insights esthetics. He also held that one should learn how to subordinate one's choices to supremely beautiful ideals. He called such knowledge ethics. And he taught that one should also reach an insight into how to think clearly about making wise choices. He called the study of sound thinking logic. The operational procedures which Peirce assigns to the three normative sciences of esthetics, ethics, and logic coincide with those which structure affective, moral, and intellectual conversion.[21] The affectively converted individual needs to understand the laws of healthy emotional development. The morally converted individual needs to know how to incarnate moral values in complex human situations. And the intellectually converted individual needs to understand the laws of sound thinking. Logic informs the other two normative sciences by providing them with the logical and methodological principles they need to advance. Thus Peirce's theory of normative sciences suggests a second dynamic within an integral conversion experience. Intellectual conversion ought to inform the other three moments in the conversion process by enabling one to think clearly about responsible emotional, moral, and religious development and about thinking itself.[21]

A third dynamic structures the conversion process: religious conversion transvalues the other forms of conversion by providing a novel faith context for interpreting their significance. Affective, intellectual, and moral conversion can occur in abstraction from the realities and ideals disclosed in God's self-revelation in Jesus and the Holy Spirit. In the normal course of adult development a particular individual may legitimately decide to cultivate healthy emotional attitudes, sound beliefs, and morally responsible patterns of behavior independently of the word of God spoken to us in the historical missions of Jesus and his Spirit. John Dewey's esthetics, ethics, and logic all illustrate the kind of natural conversion of which I speak. *Art as Experience* offers sound insights into the role of feeling in human creativity. *Human Nature and Conduct* together with Dewey's other moral and political writings illumine the way responsible moral choices are reached. *Logic: The Theory of Inquiry* yields many normative insights into the laws of sound thinking. None of

---

[21] Vincent G. Potter, S.J., *Charles S. Peirce on Norms and Ideals* (Worcester: Univ. of Massachusetts, 1967); C. S. Peirce, *Collected Papers*, ed. Charles Hartshorne and Paul Weiss (Cambridge: Harvard Univ., 1934) 6.452–93.

these works invokes gospel values or faith in a self-revealing God, but all three give evidence of having been written by a man who had experienced affective, moral, and intellectual conversion.

When conversion occurs in abstraction from divine revelation, it needs to be transformed and transvalued by religious conversion. Religious conversion effects the transvaluation of the other three forms of conversion by providing a context of faith which modifies the way in which they transpire and develop. Of itself, moral conversion demands the practical incarnation of sound ethical values in concrete decisions. Christian conversion demands that moral choices also be informed by gospel values. Of itself, affective conversion demands a confrontation with one's disordered affections and the cultivation of healthy ones. Christian conversion transforms affective conversion into repentance before God and into cultivation of Christian hope in the dark night of the senses. Christian conversion demands in addition that one go about the process of fixing one's beliefs in prayerful openness to the enlightenment of the Holy Spirit. For the Christian convert, therefore, a third dynamic structures the conversion process: the ongoing transvaluation of affective, intellectual, and moral conversion, especially when these have transpired in abstraction from divine revelation.[22]

In addition, we must distinguish initial from ongoing conversion. Initial conversion effects the transition from irresponsible to responsible behavior in emotional, speculative, moral, and religious matters. Ongoing conversion demands that one continue to confront responsibly the lived consequences of that initial conversion.

II

This construct of conversion allows one to begin to come to terms with some of the inadequacies and inauthenticities that mar both revivalistic and popular Roman Catholic piety. Revivalistic piety has traditionally suffered from both fundamentalism and rigorism. Popular Roman Catholic piety has suffered from legalism and ritual formalism. All four aberrations bespeak the absence of conversion at some level. Fundamentalism and rigorism suggest an absence of affective, intellectual, and moral conversion. They occur commonly enough when religious piety roots itself too exclusively in feeling; for when judgments of feeling succumb to neurosis, they ossify into arbitrary, authoritarian pronouncements. In speculative matters this sad process breeds suspicion of speculative criticism and fundamentalistic oversimplifications of religious faith. In moral matters it breeds the doctrinaire rigidity of the Moral Majority. Religious legalism also bespeaks an absence of both moral and religious conversion; for if the theories of Lawrence Kohlberg hold water,

---

[22] For a fuller discussion of these questions, see Gelpi, *Experiencing God* 174 ff.

the law-and-order conscience has yet to advance beyond conventional morality to autonomous (i.e., converted) moral behavior.[23] Moreover, the legalistic moralist has yet to discover the moral freedom in faith to which the Pauline epistles summon us. And empty formalistic ritual worship can conceal an absence of conversion at every level.

In its worst expressions, the Catholic charismatic renewal illustrates how the inauthenticities present in popular expressions of revivalism and Roman Catholicism can mutually reinforce one another. Certainly, charismatic Catholics of authoritarian bent have found the transition from a rigidly conservative Roman Catholic dogmatism to biblical fundamentalism all too easy. In charismatic circles the sexism that sometimes mars Roman church discipline finds a ready rationalization in fundamentalistic interpretations of a Pauline theology of headship. And both conservative charismatics and rigorists of revivalistic bent too often indulge in the same ethical oversimplifications as the Moral Majority.[24]

In its best expressions, however, the charismatic renewal also illustrates how authentic elements present in both the Roman Catholic and revivalistic traditions can mutually enrich one another. My own involvement in charismatic prayer dates from 1968, when I received the gift of tongues alone in a chapel on the campus of Fordham University. I attended my first charismatic prayer meeting almost a year later, at a national conference for the charismatic renewal held on the Notre Dame campus. I subsequently participated for three years in a prayer group that met on the campus of Loyola University in New Orleans, where I had been assigned to teach philosophy. I have since been active in prayer communities in the San Francisco Bay Area.

When I was in New Orleans, every Friday night several hundred traditional Catholics, the majority of them students, gathered for worship in a charismatic prayer group. From the beginning the pastoral leaders of the group were concerned to integrate charismatic with sacramental worship.

At the time theologians were debating the legitimacy of replacing the term "transubstantiation" with two other equally obscure theologisms: "transignification" and "transfinalization." Liturgical planning committees were experimenting with gimmicks to make the Eucharist interesting and relevant to apparently apathetic congregations. Catholic traditionalists were complaining that the new liturgical reforms had succeeded only in dissipating the feeling of mystery they had experienced at the old Latin Mass.

In our prayer group we knew the presence of Christ in our Eucharists,

[23] Lawrence Kohlberg, *Essays on Moral Development* (San Francisco: Harper and Row, 1981).

[24] Cf. Gelpi, *Charism and Sacrament* 1–24.

because we experienced it in the spontaneous prayer, personal witness, and visible giftedness of the members of our community. That experience made me begin to wonder whether the transignification debate amounted to anything more than a squabble over words.[25] I personally favor the intelligent pastoral adaptation of the liturgy, but in our prayer group we felt no need for liturgical gimmickry, because we knew from experience that liturgy comes alive when Christians rend their hearts in repentance and open them together in community to the action of the gift-giving Spirit. Nor did the absence of Latin deprive our Eucharists of mystery. We encountered a profound mystery in charismatically transformed Eucharistic worship: not the mystification that results from linguistic unintelligibility but the paschal mystery of a community consciously and visibly transformed in the Spirit of the risen Christ.

The other sacraments also acquired more vitality and meaning when understood in the light of a shared charismatic experience and celebrated in a living charismatic community of faith. Charismatic Christians frequently pray for the "healing of memories," i.e., for the healing in faith of old psychic scars. The prayer for the healing of memories demands repentance for two reasons. If the psychic scars in need of healing have resulted from wounds inflicted by others, healing usually demands that one forgive, either for the first time or with a new kind of heartfelt sincerity, those who have caused one to suffer unjustly. If the psychic scars result from personal sinfulness, healing demands repentant acceptance of a divine forgiveness that frees one to forgive oneself for what one has done. Charismatic Christians bring both such experiences of personal faith healing to the sacrament of reconciliation. In a charismatically transformed experience of sacramental healing they understand without the need for extensive theological explanation why Jesus linked the proclamation of divine forgiveness to his own ministry of healing. Nor do they need prolonged instruction on the correct use of the revised rite. In approaching the sacrament of reconciliation charismatic Catholics are already accustomed to praying with others for healing in an atmosphere of expectant and repentant faith informed by a living biblical piety.[26]

---

[25] A more fruitful approach to the problem of the real presence of Christ in the Eucharist would (1) recognize that Trent used the term "substance" in the nontechnical sense of "reality," (2) acknowledge that Trent in its Eucharistic teaching opposes the reality of the consecrated bread and wine to its appearances, (3) distinguish three senses of the terms "reality" and "appearance," and (4) show how all three terms function in the understanding of Christ's Eucharistic presence and endow that doctrine with experiential significance. For a more detailed discussion of these points, see Gelpi, *Charism and Sacrament* 239-51.

[26] Francis MacNutt, *Healing* (Notre Dame: Ave Maria, 1974); Dennis Linn and Matthew Linn, *Healing Life's Hurts: Healing of Memories through the Five Stages of Forgiveness* (New York: Paulist, 1978), and *Deliverance Prayer* (New York; Paulist, 1980); Donald L. Gelpi, "The Ministry of Healing," in *Pentecostal Piety* (New York: Paulist, 1972) 1-58;

Similarly, the charismatic experience of physical healing through faith, prayer, and the laying on of hands spontaneously transforms the way in which charismatic Christians approach the sacrament of anointing. When I first became involved in charismatic prayer, my theological stance, being fairly liberal, was tinged by demythologizing skepticism. The presence in our prayer community of physical, sometimes miraculous healing made me realize that demythologization has its limits. Moreover, when the members of our prayer group brought to the rite of anointing the same expectant faith that they brought to spontaneous prayers for physical healing, the sacrament of the sick ceased to be the ritual *coup de grâce* that it had become in traditional Catholic piety. Instead the rite took on the healing significance that theologians were beginning anew to ascribe to it.

Charismatic prayer also transforms spontaneously the way in which its practitioners approach the vocational sacraments of matrimony and orders. As I ministered to young charismatics in New Orleans, I noticed that they tended to take for granted that Christian marriage can be legitimately undertaken only in response to the anointing and call of the Spirit of Jesus. They spontaneously prayed their way toward a matrimonial commitment in a wider discerning community whose confirmation of their call to marriage they both valued and sought. Having experienced the joy of sharing the gifts of the Spirit in community, they looked forward to creating a life together animated by the same kind of shared prayer. They committed themselves to one another in a rite of marriage out of a conscious sense that their mutual love had been sanctioned both by the Spirit of Jesus and by the community of faith to which they belonged. Seminarians who have participated in and ministered to charismatic communities while preparing for ordination know what it means to be nurtured into ordained ministry by a community of faith that actively sanctions one's call to public leadership in the Church. Many priests have testified that they have rediscovered the meaning of priesthood by ministering to charismatic Christians; for they have experienced that the priesthood of the ordained finds its fulfilment in summoning the Christian community to claim their own priesthood by ministering charismatically to one another and to their ordained leaders.

Finally, from their experience of shared, Spirit-filled prayer, charismatic Christians know a truth that academic theologians are beginning to appropriate through a more painstaking and laborious scholarship: the rite of Christian initiation is a prayer for Spirit baptism.[27]

Charism and Sacrament, 81–91, 187–201, 207–12; Philippe Rouillard, O.S.B., "Le ministre du sacrement de l'onction des malades," *NRT* 101 (1979) 395–402.

[27] Raymond Schwarger, S.J., "Wassertaufe, ein Gebet um die Geisttaufe," *ZKT* 100 (1978) 36–68.

I here use the term "Spirit baptism" in the sense in which it was originally used in the Synoptics rather than in the impoverished, fundamentalistic interpretation placed upon it in classical Protestant Pentecostalism. The Synoptic Evangelists, including Luke, intended by the term a much richer and more complex experience of religious transformation in faith than just the reception of the gift of tongues. In all three Synoptic Gospels Spirit baptism reveals the purpose of ritual baptism by strengthening Jesus' disciples to bear witness to him even under persecution and by conforming their lives to his teaching. Properly understood, Spirit baptism encompasses the entire process of gracious transformation in God from initial faith to final resurrection. It includes repentance, hope, faith, love, ongoing sanctification, and mutual service in response to the charismatic anointing of the Holy Spirit. Charismatic Catholics who have discovered such experiences through shared charismatic prayer have correctly identified them as the graces promised in the rites of Christian initiation.

Indeed, much contemporary theological embarrassment over the purpose of the rite of confirmation results from the fact that many sacramental theorists are attempting to redefine the ritual's purpose in abstraction from the experiences that give it meaning and significance.[28] Judged in the light of its history, confirmation is best understood not as a separate sacrament but as a second moment in the process of Christian initiation. Baptism focuses on the death and resurrection of Jesus and invokes the Spirit to teach the neophyte to live as a child of God in the image of His Son. Baptism, therefore, ritualizes an experience of initial and ongoing repentance and conversion which bears fruit in a heart transformed by Christian hope, a mind transformed by Christian faith, and a will transformed by Christian love. Because the graces of baptism span a lifetime, the sacrament also summons the initiated Christian to lifelong docility to the Spirit in putting on the mind of Jesus by prayerfully responding to the gifts (dona) of the Holy Spirit.

Confirmation focuses attention on the experience of Pentecost when the Spirit began to effect the visible, prophetic transformation of the Christian community through an outpouring of gifts of prayer and of service. As a consequence, the rite of confirmation summons the initiated Christian to live in lifelong openness to whatever charisms of prayer and of service the Spirit may choose to give. The religious commitment demanded by confirmation differs from baptism in its specificity. All Christians are summoned to conversion, faith, hope, love, and ongoing

[28] Joseph Martos, *Doors to the Sacred* (New York: Doubleday, 1981) 205–30; Murphy Center for Liturgical Research, *Made Not Born: New Perspectives on Christian Initiation and the Catechumenate* (Notre Dame: Univ. of Notre Dame, 1976).

sanctification in the image of Jesus and the power of his Spirit; and all are called to lifelong receptivity to some gift of service in the Christian community. But not every Christian receives the same service gift; for since the ordinary charisms of the Spirit effect the gracious transformation of the human ego, we may count as many different gifts of service as there are different graced human personalities. Because the commitment to respond to a particular gift of service differs in its specificity from the commitment common to all Christians to respond to the sanctifying Spirit in repentant faith, hope, and love, the two commitments legitimately constitute two different ritual moments in the process of Christian initiation and can be appropriately symbolized in two different ritual acts.[29]

III

All Christians are, then, called through the rites of initiation to live in lifelong, charismatic openness to the Spirit. Inevitably, therefore, the designation of a particular movement in the Church as "charismatic" breeds a host of potentially serious confusions and misunderstandings. It falsely suggests that only those Christians who attend prayer meetings deserve the name "charismatic." In point of fact, all Christians are called to live charismatically, and those who fail to respond to the Spirit's charisms of sanctification and of service introduce serious inauthenticity into their religious commitment.

Similarly, if one designates only those who attend prayer meetings as "charismatic," one also fallaciously implies that only those acts which transpire within the context of a "charismatic" prayer meeting merit being called "charismatic." The charismatic renewal is certainly restoring gifts of feeling, of healing, of prophecy, and of prayer to the Catholic community as a whole, gifts that have been popularly neglected for centuries. But charismatic prayer groups often reflect both the limitations and the strengths of classical Pentecostal piety. Classical Pentecostal spirituality tends to turn inward rather than to deal with political and economic issues of faith and justice; and when fundamentalistic it misprizes speculative theology. In point of fact, many charisms of service like helping, administration, practical care of the poor, community leadership, etc. cannot be exercised in the context of shared charismatic prayer. When, therefore, one limits the term "charismatic" to what goes on in prayer groups, one fallaciously absolves Christians from serving others in prayerful docility to the Spirit's charismatic anointing. When Christians fail to recognize their charismatic status, they tend all too often to obey natural or sinful ego drives rather than the graced leading

---

[29] Gelpi, *Charism and Sacrament* 1-156; *Unitatis redintegratio* 22: *Lumen gentium* 12.

of the Spirit. They fail to name the charismatic movements of the Spirit in their lives as gracious inspirations. Through their consequent failure to testify publicly and explicitly to the Spirit's anointing, they diminish the shared faith consciousness of the Christian community not through action but through ignorance, apathy, and omission.

Several other popular misunderstandings of the term "charism" stand in the way of a systematic theological reappropriation of the charismatic basis of authentic sacramental worship. Among them the following should be named. Max Weber has popularized the misleading notion that the charismatic and the institutional stand irreconcilably opposed in principle. Charismatic impulses are often stereotyped as enthusiastic and mindlessly emotional. The charismatic is slandered as a marginal, esoteric, optional strain in Christian piety, tolerable perhaps for those who can tolerate it but a nonessential appendage to solid Christian devotion. The charismatic is also fallaciously equated with the unusual, the extraordinary, or the miraculous. Let us reflect on each of these misunderstandings in turn.

In Pauline theology a "charism" (*charisma*) signifies a particular manifestation of the grace (*charis*) bestowed upon us by God through Jesus Christ and in his Spirit.[30] Far from being opposed to institutional ministry, the charisms underpin and authenticate administration and official church leadership. When, therefore, personal charism and institutional structures seem to conflict, the conflict results not from the charismatic anointing of the Spirit but from human egotism and from unconverted, vested institutional interests.

While some charisms, like prophecy and gifts of prayer, address the heart, others, like evangelization and instruction, address the mind as well. Others still, like gifts of discernment, helping, and practical leadership, seek to inspire decisions that foster the community's growth in faith. Not every charism, therefore, speaks primarily to the human emotions. A sound charismatic piety preserves a healthy balance among feeling, thought, and action.[31]

Nor should the charismatic action of the Spirit be caricatured as marginal, esoteric, or optional. As we have seen, Christian conversion begins with a repentant confrontation with one's own sinfulness and culminates in the decision to live as a child of God in the image of Jesus. Authentic Christian conversion inaugurates a life lived in conformity with the teaching of Jesus. Jesus, however, summons his followers to a

[30] John Koenig, *Charismata: God's Gifts for God's People* (Philadelphia: Westminster, 1978); George Montague, S.M., *The Holy Spirit: Growth of a Biblical Tradition* (New York: Paulist, 1976) 127–228; B. N. Wanbacam, O.Praem., "Le mot 'charisme,'" *NRT* 97 (1975) 345–55.

[31] Gelpi, *Experiencing God* 205–58.

faith in the providence of God that frees them to share their bread with others. He calls them to practical concern for the neediest and for the marginal and outcast members of society. He demands that mutual forgiveness in love attest the authenticity of his disciples' prayer. Moreover, all this the followers of Jesus must do in response to the sanctifying Spirit with whom he baptizes them. In other words, those who profess to follow Jesus commit themselves to life in a community of faith sharing and mutual forgiveness. Moreover, the Spirit who bonds us to one another in community also calls each Christian to some form of practical service of others in the name and image of Jesus. Any service undertaken in response to the Spirit's anointing deserves to be called a *charisma* no matter how ordinary or quotidian; for it manifests the gracing activity of the Spirit of Christ. Lifelong openness to the gifts of sanctification and of service follows, therefore, as an unavoidable consequence of authentic conversion to Christ. Far from being marginal, esoteric, or optional, the charisms specify every Christian call to service; for every converted Christian is called to a pentecostal moment when growth in sanctity matures into a clear sense of the way one is called to serve others practically in Jesus' name.[32]

Nor need such service be confined to the unusual or the extraordinary. An extraordinary gift like the gift of miracles lacks any clear foundation in the talents and abilities of those who exercise it. Most charisms transform the way in which we exercise our natural gifts by endowing that exercise with prayerful receptivity to the anointing and illumination of the Spirit. Failure to value the ordinary gifts of the Spirit can breed charismania, or obsessive preoccupation with the preternatural and the miraculous. But charismania neurotically distorts a sound charismatic piety into an aberration. Authentic charismatic piety can find God in all things, even in the ordinary.

IV

Once one concedes that visible charismatic transformation in the Spirit ought to be a result of any authentic Christian conversion, one can also use C. S. Peirce's pragmatic maxim in order to clarify not only the dynamics of Christian conversion but also the inseparability of charismatic prayer from authentic sacramental worship. Peirce's maxim states in labored prose: "The entire intellectual purport of any symbol consists in the total of all general modes of rational conduct which, conditionally upon all the possible different circumstances and desires, would ensue upon the acceptance of the symbol."[33] Inadequate as a definition of meaning, the pragmatic maxim, when systematically applied to a theology

---

[32] Gelpi, *Charism and Sacrament* 1–156; *Experiencing God* 259–321.
[33] C. S. Peirce, *Collected Papers* 5.438.

of conversion, nevertheless produces clarifying results. For example, when we invoke the maxim to explore the charismatic consequences of Christian initiation, we begin to understand why the seven sacramental rites of the Church can legitimately be called a system. They are dynamically ordered to one another through the charismatic activity of the Spirit of Jesus. Let us draw on the preceding reflections in order to understand how this occurs.

As we have just seen, among the practical consequences of Christian conversion we must number the willingness to live in lifelong responsiveness to the Spirit's charismatic call to faith sharing and to mutual service in community. One enters the Christian community through the rites of initiation. In the case of adults, sacramental initiation seals an experience of initial conversion and introduces one to ongoing conversion. In the case of infants, it introduces the baptized child into a community that seeks to lead it to just such an adult conversion experience. In either case, the Spirit's sanctifying gifts and charismatic call to service number among the fundamental graces of the rites of initiation. The sanctifying action of the Spirit flows especially from the baptismal moment in sacramental initiation; for baptism conforms us to Jesus by summoning us to incarnate in our moral decisions the religious values he lived and proclaimed. The call to mutual service in community flows in a special way from confirmation, which recalls the beginning of the Spirit's visible, charismatic transformation of the Church on Pentecost day. Confirmation summons the confirmed Christian to lifelong openness to whatever call to service the Spirit might summon.

Two of the Spirit's calls to service in community demand sacramental confirmation: marriage and orders. Indeed, one can argue that the sacramental character of both rituals derives in part from the fact that both lend official public sanction to a particular charism of service within the Christian community.

Reconciliation and anointing under present sacramental discipline ritualize the healing ministry of the ordained; for in proclaiming the word of God to the Christian community, the ordained summon believers to ongoing repentance and conversion. Every efficacious proclamation of the word ought to be accompanied by efficacious signs of healing. That healing assumes different forms: initial and ongoing conversion itself, the transformation of suffering into grace, or the complete, sometimes miraculous removal of suffering. As we have seen, the sacrament of reconciliation ritualizes the ongoing conversion of the baptized. The sacrament of anointing effects either the transformation of suffering into grace or the complete removal of some physical or psychic illness. Both rites, therefore, engage gifts, or charisms, of healing.

Finally, Eucharistic worship ritualizes the ongoing reaffirmation of one's covenant of initiation. Since, however, the initiated Christian stands committed to respond to the Spirit's sanctifying gifts and charismatic call to service, the extent to which any given Christian community lives in practical openness to the Spirit's charisms measures the authenticity of its Eucharistic worship.

Clearly, the application of Peirce's practical logic of consequences to sacramental worship casts light on the dynamic, charismatic unity of the sacramental system. It also clarifies the practical meaning of the term "primordial sacramentality" (*Ursakrament*). The term emerged from an attempt to apply existential phenomenology to sacramental theology. Having rejected an Aristotelian causal analysis of the sacraments as "ontic," existential sacramentalists tried through descriptive methods to discover deeper ontological structures of meaning within sacramental worship. The Incarnation was described as the primordial sacrament of existential encounter with a self-revealing God, and the Church as a primordial sacrament that mysteriously prolongs that original act of divine self-revelation in space and time. The seven sacraments were seen as ritual explicitations of this more fundamental primordial sacramentality.[34]

But when these theological abstractions were used to interpret a contemporary experience of sacramental worship, they sometimes rang hollow. Worshiping Christians did not always experience their local parish as a primordial sacrament. Complaints surfaced in more than one place about the tedium, sterility, and superficiality of sacramental worship. These expressions of dissatisfaction effectively dramatized the fact that sacramental theology needs more than phenomenology to discover the primordial sacramentality of the Christian community. Phenomenology can only describe what appears. But the saving presence of God will appear in a community of worship only if its members are actively responding to the Spirit's charismatic call to sanctification and to service by putting on the mind of Jesus and by serving one another in the ways the Spirit prompts; for one can describe the primordial sacramentality of a Christian community only if it has been evoked from the community by an efficacious word of proclamation that summons its members to repentance, living faith, ongoing sanctification, and mutual charismatic service. In other words, sacramental theology will fail to offer an adequate account of primordial sacramentality if it uses descriptive methods only. Sacramentalists also need to engage in normative thinking about the kinds of behavior which endow the shared faith experience of any given

[34] For a more detailed discussion of this point, see Gelpi, *Charism and Sacrament* 97–110.

community with primordial sacramentality. The application of pragmatic logic to a theology of conversion offers the kind of normative thinking sacramental theology needs.

Theological reflection on the religious experience of charismatic Catholics suggests, therefore, that a sound and balanced charismatic piety has the capacity to effect the renewal of sacramental worship from within. Even more, it suggests that sacramental worship which fails to celebrate the charismatic action of the Spirit of Jesus in the Christian community suffers from serious inauthenticity. This conclusion should give many Catholics, both clerical and lay, pause; for Spirit-consciousness and a conscious cultivation of the charisms has not dominated Roman Catholic piety for centuries. The fact remains, however, that living faith in the Holy Spirit (as opposed to the bare doctrinal affirmation that the Spirit exists as a member of the Trinity) demands conscious and practical openness to the Spirit's call of sanctification and to all the charisms of prayer and of service from tongues to ordained leadership.

V

Contemporary charismatic piety offers other pastoral challenges and opportunities as well. The charismatic renewal, like other revivals before it, fosters grass-roots ecumenism; and history teaches that without grass-roots support the ecumenical labors of theologians and of church leaders are foredoomed to frustration. Two councils—Lyons II and Florence—labored to reunite Eastern and Western Christians. Both failed for lack of grass-roots preparation and support. Contemporary ecumenical dialogue will founder on the same rock unless the pastoral leaders of the churches find ways to shatter denominational complacency and inspire a desire for union among ordinary Christians.

The charismatic renewal provides a variety of opportunities for Christians of different denominations to share their faith and their experience of Jesus and of the Spirit. Shared charismatic prayer shatters denominational stereotypes by fostering a spontaneous, personal witness to God that dramatizes a shared faith bonding Christians despite denominational differences. Charismatic Christians of different churches have collaborated in sponsoring Jesus rallies and similar ecumenical equivalents of the old Eucharistic Congresses. They have participated in workshops on Christian prayer and spirituality. But the most potent motive which shared charismatic prayer provides for fostering grass-roots ecumenism is the experience of shared prayer itself. Spirit-inspired prayer breeds love. Only when Christians of different denominations learn to love one another will they begin to feel separation as painful.

Divisions in any community of faith betoken an absence of conversion at some level: affective, intellectual, moral, or religious. Blind prejudice, mutual misunderstanding, apathy in the face of the social, economic, and political challenges of contemporary society, rote or compartmentalized religion—these and similar attitudes divide the churches. The charismatic renewal cannot claim to be the only effective way of fostering grass-roots ecumenism; but it does demand conversion, openness to the Spirit, and shared prayer as the preconditions for ecumenical contact. As a consequence, it creates a climate in which the divisions which separate Christians can be dealt with prayerfully, lovingly, and in obedience to the Spirit.[35]

The need for conversion poses a second challenge to charismatic Christians and to the churches. Any Christian who claims to be Spirit-baptized must accept the moral consequences of commitment to Jesus as the normative historical revelation of who God is and what we humans are called to become. Those who claim Jesus as Lord must submit to the constraints of discipleship; and discipleship, as all four Gospels insist, exacts a high cost. Jesus summons his followers to a trust in the Father's providential care that frees them to share whatever they have with others on the basis not of merit but of need. He demands mutual forgiveness as the most fundamental test of the authenticity of worship.

We Americans live in a country that consumes an enormous and disproportionate amount of the world's resources. We live under an administration that subordinates human rights abroad to American economic interests. We waste billions of dollars creating weapons of nuclear destruction while millions of humans starve. For the contemporary Christian, one crucial test of moral and religious conversion must remain the ability to name these forces as antichrist; for the Christian convert who refuses to confront the principalities and powers of this world and summon them to repentance and to the obedience of faith succumbs to hypocrisy and inauthenticity.

The history of revivalism in this country suggests that soon or late it becomes politicized. Although some might be inclined to regard the Moral Majority and other similar groups as ethically inauthentic offshoots of contemporary American revivalism, unlike previous revivals the charismatic renewal has yet to undergo systematic politicization. But the potential exists. Nuclear disarmament and world hunger confront the American Church as moral issues of such enormous consequence that those who choose to ignore them sin by omission. Pastoral leaders of charismatic communities need to join their voices to the growing number of bishops and other Christians who seek to transform the Catholic community into a church of peace advocacy committed to the elimination

[35] Kilian McDonnell, *The Charismatic Renewal and Ecumenism* (New York: Paulist, 1978); Paul Lebeau, S.J., "The Charismatic Renewal and Ecumenism," *Lumen vitae* 31 (1976) 171–85; Gelpi, *Pentecostal Piety* 61–80.

of world hunger. Active participation in Christian lobbies like Bread for the World or Pax Christi offers one concrete way of bringing political pressure to bear to shape national policy in ways that lead to peace and to justice. Only time will tell whether the religious enthusiasm generated by this latest American revival will attempt to suffuse the political search for both peace and justice with authentic religious fervor. If it does, it will have advanced the inculturation of the gospel in this country in a significant way.

WILLIAM C. SPOHN

The Reasoning Heart: An American Approach to Christian Discernment

WILLIAM C. SPOHN, S.J., teaches moral theology at the Jesuit
School of Theology at Berkeley. He specializes in Scripture
and ethics as well as in American theology and moral
philosophy. He is the author of *What Are They Saying about
Scripture and Ethics?*

MAKING MORAL decisions is as common an experience as walking and as difficult to analyze. Physiologists despair of providing a full description of the interplay of nerve, muscle, tendon, and bone that comprises walking. Moral philosophers rarely attempt to delineate the processes which lead to moral decisions. Fortunately, most people manage both operations with some degree of success despite the lack of a descriptive rationale. However, rapid cultural change and social instability can confuse moral decision-making just as a slight malfunction of the inner ear can ruin a person's balance. In such periods of confusion greater attention needs to be given to examining the actual practice of moral agents.

"Discernment" plays a central role in making moral decisions. It is the skill of moral evaluation in the concrete. It employs symbolic and affective criteria to accomplish this evaluation. When taken in a religious context, discernment connotes a graced ability to detect what is the appropriate response to the invitation of God. It goes beyond the question "Is this action morally right?" to the more personal question of appropriateness: "Is this action consistent with who I am and want to become? What sort of person does this type of action?" Abstractions are less helpful here than the resources of memory and imagination.[1]

Moral philosophers and theologians do not usually consider the processes of discernment, the use of symbols and affectivity to find the personally fitting course of action. They concentrate on justification of decisions rather than on their initial formulation. It is doubtless important to give publicly intelligible reasons for what we have decided; but it

[1] "'Discernment' seems to be appropriate for pointing to the ability to distinguish the important from the unimportant information and the insightful interpretations from the uninsightful. It refers to the ability to perceive relationships between aspects of the information that enables one to see how it all fits together, or how it cannot fit together. It refers to the ability to suggest inferences that can be drawn from the information, and thus to an imaginative capacity" (James M. Gustafson, Theology and Christian Ethics [Philadelphia: Pilgrim, 1974] 104).

would be misleading to imply that we must make our decisions in the same logical way that we justify them. Moral theologians have often used the practical syllogism in framing their arguments: moral principle was applied to relevant case to yield a moral conclusion about action. However, do we actually *make* our decisions by the practical syllogism? An exclusively rational moral agent might do so, but ordinary mortals perceive and evaluate their situation in a more complex fashion.

In this discussion I will refer to this neglected aspect of moral experience by the term "the reasoning heart." If Pascal was correct in assigning the heart its own distinctive reasons, then we should determine the moral capacities of memory and imagination. The "heart" refers to the agent as engaged, as a being of vision and feeling. In biblical morality it is the seat of affectivity and virtuous qualities. The heart refers to the moral agent in his or her particularity, as a definite character with a specific sense of identity and set of dispositions. Discernment is precisely this reasoning of the heart.

Discernment should not be set in opposition to the "reasoning head," to abstract reasoning with general moral principles. We need not be as pessimistic as Pascal that reason is oblivious to the reasons of the heart. The concrete judgments of discernment complement these general moral considerations. Discernment operates within the boundaries set by general principles of justice, honesty, and the like. Discernment attends to the particular situation, illuminating its meaning for this agent and indicating what response is appropriate. It makes *judgments of affectivity* which are based upon central convictions of the person's character. These are open to their own kind of scrutiny. It is a different scrutiny from the formal logic which tests out the general judgments of morality which we will call *judgments of rationality*. Just because discernment is personal does not imply that it is private: the aesthetic judgments of affectivity are accountable to symbolic and affective criteria which are derived from public traditions.

Situation ethics and intuitionism make the mistake of opposing concrete judgments of affectivity to general norms of morality. Judgments of rationality are necessary in morality to set the boundary conditions for action and to provide reasons for conduct which are publicly intelligible. Training in sound moral reasoning can help the agent detect logical and unwarranted exceptions to norms. However, another set of skills is necessary to become a discerning person. This article will argue that discernment can be scrutinized by attending to the central symbols which shape self-understanding and to the dominant affective convictions which dispose the self to action. The Christian tradition offers certain normative symbols and patterns to affectivity which can serve as criteria for Christian discernment. These symbols and affections are correlated with the fundamental religious convictions about God and Jesus Christ. Therefore, while discernment is a personal skill like prudence, it need not be strictly private but should also be accountable to the public convictions of the Christian tradition.[2]

Karl Rahner has provided one of the most widely accepted accounts of Christian discernment. He analyzes the Spirtual Exercises of Ignatius of Loyola to determine how concrete courses of action can have a religious significance, an indication of divine calling. In subsequent applications Rahner suggests that Christian discernment may be at the core of the assent of faith and should become central to the pastoral task of moral theology. He proposes training the laity in an "existential ethics" which can perceive God's invitations in the concrete situations of politics and economy in order to supplement the traditional "essential ethics" of natural law.[3]

However, Rahner has not given sufficient attention to the role of religious symbols and affectivity in guiding sound discernment. This article will argue that a more adequate account of Christian discernment may be derived from American theologians, particularly Jonathan Edwards and H. Richard Niebuhr. They provide a richer analysis of the moral agent, extend discernment to a critical reading of the signs of the times, and also incorporate biblical material into the act of discernment more adequately than does Rahner. All three theologians suppose that God is active in history and enters the experience of men and women. God's intentions for the world and individuals are not only to be found in the general structures of creation and universal moral principles. For the Christian the moral question "What ought I to do?" needs to be preceded by a more fundamental question: "What is God enabling and requiring me to do?" To answer the question, the Christian must always engage in serious discernment.[4]

SYMBOLIC CRITERIA FOR DISCERNMENT

The first criteria for discernment are the symbols which guide its evaluation of the concrete situation. Judgments of affectivity, the conclusions of the reasoning heart, are felt to be appropriate both to who I am

[2] See Louise M. Des Marais, *Signs of Glory: Making Christian Choices* (Denville, N.J.: Dimension, 1975).

[3] Cf. Karl Rahner, *The Dynamic Element in the Church* (New York: Herder and Herder, 1964) chap. 3, "The Logic of Concrete Individual Knowledge in Ignatius Loyola"; *The Spiritual Exercises of St. Ignatius* (tr. Louis J. Puhl; Westminster, Md.: Newman, 1963); Karl Rahner, "On the Question of a Formal Existential Ethics," *Theological Investigations* (hereafter *TI*) 2 (Baltimore: Helicon, 1963), 217–34.

[4] "Theologically, it might be said that God is enabling men to discern what God is enabling men to do; but the locus for discernment is in the self as it relates beliefs about the God in whom it trusts to the situation in which it acts" (Gustafson, *Theology* 115).

and what I am responding to. Karl Rahner tests possible responses
against a basic sense of the self. Niebuhr clarifies this by analyzing the
basic symbols which shape the individual's self-understanding and the
symbols the agent uses to interpret the situation. While Rahner analyzes
the moment of individual consciousness to discover the structure of
discernment, Niebuhr brings the history of the person to bear on the
process, thus utilizing the symbolic resources of imagination, memory,
and the Christian tradition.

Rahner notes that traditional spirituality recognized that Christians
can receive particular calls from God, vocations which are not simply the
application of general moral norms and values. These are not only calls
to a particular state in life, such as marriage or ordination, but also to
specific courses of action. Traditional moral theology had difficulty in
explaining the serious sense of obligation which accompanied these
vocations. How could one person be obliged to do something when
another individual faced with the same choice would experience no moral
obligation at all?

In these vocation experiences the will of God is not discovered by
appealing to general moral principles. In fact, these material norms of
"essential ethics" are presupposed. An "existential ethics" which will
examine the formal structure of vocation experiences to test their authenticity must complement essential ethics.

Most people come to serious decisions in a manner that is quite similar
to the ordinary process of discernment in the Spiritual Exercises.

> In such decisions a man thinks things over for a long time. Consequently in
> every case he will probably make his decisions through a fundamental global
> awareness of himself actually present and making itself felt in him during this
> space of time, and through a feeling of the harmony or disharmony of the object
> of choice with this fundamental feeling he has about himself. He will not only
> nor ultimately make his decision by a rational analysis but by whether he feels
> that something "suits him" or not. And this feeling will be judged by whether the
> matter pleases, delights, brings peace and satisfaction.[5]

Rahner has outlined the formal structure of the experience of discernment; the options facing the person are tested against the global awareness of the self. The criteria used are not logical but aesthetic, because
peace, radical satisfaction, and delight are the signs which determine
which option harmonizes with the sense of self. The right option is not
only morally correct; it also is the most appropriate one, the one most
consistent with the kind of person the agent is and aspires to become.

Rahner fails to explain how each person has this "fundamental sense
of self" that is unique. Instead, he focuses on a certain kind of religious

---

[5] Rahner, *Dynamic Element* 166.

experience. This is the experience of radical receptivity to God, a non-conceptual awareness of God, who is the goal of human reaching out to infinity. This orientation to God as mystery constitutes for Rahner the core of every human person. The test of discernment is precisely this "experience of transcendence as such."[6] If a proposed course of action harmonizes with this central religious attitude, then it is recognized as the will of God for the person. The end will indicate what is the most appropriate means. Here the end is God Himself, who is present in the person's longing and hope. The most apt means to the end are determined by a judgment of affectivity. The means will harmonize with this radical longing for God, while inappropriate courses of action will stifle and obscure this reaching out to God.[7] This process of discerning the means presumes that the end is actually present, that conversion has occurred to the extent that God is the final value of the person's life. Only such a person would have been able to make the Spiritual Exercises.

This sense of self is difficult to locate in our consciousness. The awareness of self which accompanies our every thought cannot itself be expressed conceptually. When we focus on who we are, our cognitive description never measures up to the full reality. Hence Rahner describes this as an "unthematic" awareness, since it cannot be adequately thematized or comprehended directly.[8] It remains a sense, an awareness that is concomitant to all our conscious experiences. Can such an elusive sense serve the role of criterion in practical discernment?

American theologians have also employed the self as a basic norm in moral reflection, but they have a richer notion of the self than Rahner. He focuses on radical freedom and "transcendence" as the core of the self, while their description points to the unique history which has formed the individual. That history is present to the discerning person through memories and symbols which form his or her identity. The pattern of God's previous action in the person's life can therefore become a more central part of discerning the immediate situation. Rahner concentrates on the moment of discernment, like one freezing a moving picture to examine a single frame of film. Considering the personal history and social context of the person would be like viewing the film progressively

---

[6] Ibid. 139. Accordingly, "the operative principle of choice will be God, or, more precisely, that concrete, unique, intrinsic orientation to God which constitutes the innermost essence of man, emerging actually into awareness in operation and active accomplishment ... " (ibid. 160).

[7] "For the freely accepted transcendent experience of the Spirit is only possible here and now through concentration upon one distinct object of choice among others. This means that this object does not in any way lessen or distort the experience of the Spirit but rather provides a concrete and practical means of expression for it" (Rahner, "Experience of the Spirit and Existential Commitment," *TI* 16, 32).

[8] Karl Rahner, *Foundations of Christian Faith* (New York: Seabury, 1978) chap. 1.

up to this moment, thereby providing a richer framework for discernment. What is needed is a fuller phenomenology of moral character than Rahner offers, a description which sees the self emerging as an identity in a specific history and social context.

H. Richard Niebuhr and other American thinkers have developed a theory of the self which shows the importance of symbols in shaping personal identity. First we will examine how symbols from the Christian tradition shape the self and then we will consider how these symbols aid in discerning the signs of the times, God's call in the larger social world.

In *The Responsible Self* Niebuhr argues that the self-understanding of the moral agent is prior to questions of action.[9] Whatever answer I give to the moral question, "What ought I to do?" will be profoundly affected by my answer to the question of identity, "Who am I?" Identity rests more on images and metaphors of the self than on definite ideas. They provide pictures through which the unique character of the self can be glimpsed and they organize habitual ways of responding to the world. For example, if I feel myself to be a victim, I am likely to inject weariness and fear into even innocent relationships. My defensiveness may be all the more powerful if this image of being a victim remains unconscious. My spontaneous reactions will be defensive or even hostile, leading me to actions which are more appropriate to my fear of being violated again than to the actual situation, which may contain nothing objectively threatening. Discernment will be operating but it will be neurotic discernment, skewed by my inadequate self-image. Until this level of self-understanding is altered, it will distort my perception and evaluation of the world around me.

Christian conversion involves moral transformation precisely because it challenges the central images of the self. *Metanoia* means rethinking my personal history through a new set of images which the community proposes as normative. If I have previously conceived of myself as victim, I no longer can remember the past as a series of undeserved injuries and fear a future which will contain more of the same. Viewing myself as one who has been forgiven and empowered to forgive others, I need to reinterpret that history of injuries. Because I now believe that the cross and resurrection of Jesus will be part of my own experience, my attitude towards injury cannot be simply resentment and wariness. The events are not changed, but their meaning must be if I am to be a Christian. If the God I now believe in brought life precisely where death had seemed invincible in the experience of Christ, then I am enabled to look for life in the most threatening memories of my own past. Reinterpreted in light of the normative images of faith, my past can issue in compassion for

[9] H. Richard Niebuhr, *The Responsible Self* (New York: Harper & Row, 1963) 48.

the suffering and a new capacity for service.[10]

Most systems of ethics are incapable of describing the change of personal identity which Christian faith requires. They do not consider the moral agent in his or her particularity, but rather focus on certain aspects of the agent which are shared in common with other moral agents. Whether that common aspect be a general human nature, rationality, or logical discourse, it prescinds from the particular identity of the person. These generalizable features of the moral agent are necessary to provide the foundations of judgments of rationality in ethics—moral principles and general theories of virtue. However, they are incapable of grounding judgments of affectivity, which are the bases of discernment. A Christian ethics which only addresses judgments of rationality will consequently shed little light on the transformation of the particular person. Because human nature and rationality presumably remain the same after religious conversion, the moral life can seem largely unaffected by coming to faith.

American philosophy, with its characteristic stress on experience, offers a more promising approach to the particularity of the moral agent. Particular events become intelligible when they are located as parts in an intelligible whole. Particular persons derive their uniqueness from the contexts in which they view themselves and from the history of their own choices. For George Herbert Mead, the self is not understood substantially but interactionally. Niebuhr developed Mead's notion that the self comes into being through interaction with others. "[The] self is a being which comes to knowledge of itself in the presence of other selves ... its very nature is that of a being which lives in response to other selves."[11] The self does not have its meaning because it is an instance of human nature; the meaning of this particular self emerges through dialog with others. Therefore a new "root metaphor" is necessary for moral philosophy: the self-as-responder is more adequate to the interactional development of the self than previous root metaphors. These have been self-as-maker, which likens the moral life to a constructive quest for human happiness, and self-as-citizen, which portrays the moral life as a life of obedience to universal laws.[12]

---

[10] For an account of the conversion of affections and the reinterpretation of past experience that results, see Paul V. Robb, S.J. "Conversion as a Human Experience," *Studies in the Spirituality of Jesuits* 14/3 (1982).

[11] Niebuhr, *Responsible Self* 71.

[12] "Responder" is a synecdochic analogy, because it takes a special part of experience to envision the whole. Although it is more comprehensive than the other two images, it does not for that reason rule out moral reflection on goals and norms; its claim is to greater, not exclusive, adequacy. "Yet the understanding of ourselves as responsive beings ... is a fruitful conception, which brings into view aspects of our self-defining conduct that are obscured when the older images are exclusively employed" (ibid. 57).

The truly responsible self is not merely reactive; rather, it functions like the good conversationalist who seeks to further the dialog with others. Such a person attempts to make sense out of the previous remarks and to contribute something which makes further response possible. The bore, on the other hand, derails the conversation by using others as sounding boards for self-centered monolog. As the responsible self interacts with the larger community, it makes commitments which provide it with a sense of integrity. Josiah Royce has written that personal individuality is not a given commodity but only gradually arises as the self becomes committed to causes beyond itself.[13] Authentic Christian commitment rests on loyalty to the cause of Christ, which is universal reconciliation.

Defensiveness is a major threat to the responsible life. The very community which initially forms the self can become a parochial allegiance, setting itself over against other groups as rivals. Accountability is then limited only to the local social context as defensiveness takes the place of identification with others who are different. This constricted loyalty yields a faith which must inevitably conflict with faith in the one sovereign Lord of all humankind. The Church itself can generate this sort of parochialism, in contrast to genuine faith in Christ. Loyalty to the Church community can be Christian only if it is loyalty to a more universal community. "And even when I find that I can be responsible in the church only as I respond to Jesus Christ, I discover in him one who points beyond himself to the cause to which he is faithful and in faithfulness to which he is faithful to his companions—not the companions encountered in the church, but in the world to which the Creator is faithful, which the Creator has made his cause."[14] The responsible Christian is therefore accountable not only to the community of faith but also to the universal community and to its Lord. The universal frame of reference is the whole within which the individual finds meaning as a part.

Discernment seeks to be responsible to social contexts by aid of the images with which they shape our self-understanding. Our sense of self is defined in large part by images of being parent, citizen, colleague, friend, committee member, theologian, and the like. Niebuhr argues that a coherent sense of self depends on an ultimate loyalty which structures all the lesser loyalties: faith in one God who acts in all the events that happen to us. Christian discernment seeks to be accountable to this Lord through understanding itself in the normative symbols of revelation. And

[13] "Yet their loyalty gives them a business. It unifies their activities. It makes each of these loyal beings an individual self—a life unified by a purpose" (Josiah Royce, *The Philosophy of Loyalty* [New York: Macmillan, 1909] 170).

[14] Niebuhr, *Responsible Self* 86.

the primary "symbolic form" for understanding how to respond to God is the person of Jesus Christ.

The sense of self which guides discernment is more than a present awareness. It has been shaped over time through suffering and decision. Therefore it can only be captured in a timeful symbol, one which can display the evolving identity of the self. To appreciate this historical uniqueness, we need to move from self-image to story. The fuller answer to the question "Who am I?" must be an autobiography, a narrative which can portray the character that emerges in time. In this aspect as well as in self-images, the Christian tradition provides a normative account, namely, the story of Jesus as located within the larger story of Israel. Biblical narratives function as paradigms in discernment because they reveal challenges in the present which are analogous to those of the past.

Biblical narratives can uncover the conflict of loyalties between our old way of life and the life of faith; at the same time they encourage us on the path of this costly grace. Dorothy Day, founder of the Catholic Worker movement, wrote of the costliness of her own decision to become a Christian. She was living with a man whom she deeply loved and who was the father of her only child. However, he could not stomach institutional religion and so had insisted that she would have to choose between him and the Church. She wrote: "God always gives us a chance to show our preference for Him. With Abraham it was to sacrifice his only son. With me it was to give up my married life with Forster. You do these things blindly, not because it is your natural inclination . . . but because you wish to live in conformity with the will of God."[15]

The story of Abraham could guide her discernment because it was characteristic of the believer before God and also characteristic of the God who calls to faith today. Character cannot be portrayed through abstraction; it is glimpsed through the surprising twists and turns of the plot of a narrative. Dorothy Day could grasp more than some analogous elements between her situation and that of Abraham. She could also discern the presence of the God of Abraham, who continues to act in character. The path from quandary to resolution which shaped the faith of Abraham could be revelatory for her because it disclosed God's call and promised His faithfulness.

Stories move from one scene to another and convey the hearer from here to there. They capture the self-in-time and point towards the particular path for the self to take. Sallie McFague writes that human experience itself has a narrative quality which these paradigmatic stories of faith support. "We love stories, then, because our lives are stories and

---

[15] Dorothy Day, *The Long Loneliness* (New York: Harper, 1952) 256.

we recognize in the attempts of others to move, temporally and painfully, our own story. We recognize in the stories of others' experiences of coming to belief our own agonizing journey and we rejoice in the companionship of those on the way."[16] Our lives are stories because they have a dramatic unity that moves through time, a plot which reveals and shapes our particular character. That same dramatic unity intimates what should come next, a future coherent with what has gone before.

The story of Jesus makes a normative claim upon Christian discernment. It is not just any story, but one which claims our lives by asserting that it must be the truth of those lives. This is the story which reveals in a definitive way God's intentions for the world and for us. Christian conversion occurs when we let the story of Jesus become our story, as we let the particular shape of our lives be conformed to the particular shape of Jesus' life. The confession of faith appropriately takes a narrative form for Israel and for Christians: it is a self-involving confession to take the same journey ourselves.

Stanley Hauerwas writes that Peter's confession in Mark 8 is called into question by his subsequent reluctance to take the journey which will lead to the cross. "Jesus thus rebukes Peter, who had learned the name but not the story that determines the meaning of the name."[17] Peter projected his own worldly story of ambition and success onto the title of "the Christ." Jesus counters with the story of the cross which awaits him, and that story must change Peter. "A story that claims to be the truth of our existence requires that our lives, like the lives of the disciples, be changed by following him."[18]

The narrative of the Gospel embodies a whole way of life that is inseparable from the character of its central figure. Peter, like all of us, wanted to separate his relationship with Jesus from the threatening demands of that way of life. He wanted faith without discipleship. The Gospel narrative itself is best understood from the destiny to which it inexorably led: the cross and resurrection of Jesus. It is normative for the character of individuals and for the Church, which is the "organized form of Jesus' story."[19] The canonical Scriptures have authority for those who join this community. This does not mean that the biblical narrative is the sole source of moral wisdom but that the cross and resurrection of Christ must test moral insight from any sources. The truth of the narrative itself is manifest in the lives of the people that it forms; it cannot be

[16] Sallie McFague, *Speaking in Parables* (Philadelphia: Fortress, 1975) 138–39.
[17] Stanley Hauerwas, *A Community of Character* (Notre Dame: Univ. of Notre Dame, 1981) 48.
[18] Ibid. 47.
[19] Ibid. 50.

established without some lived participation.[20]

Discernment operates by fitting the part into a whole which illuminates the significance of the part. The sense of self of the individual gains intelligibility when its social and historical contexts provide this illumination as larger wholes. The present moment fits within the story which forms the individual's character, and that story must be appropriate to the normative context of the story of Jesus for the believer. This normative context can guide discernment by suggesting the response which best "fits in." Niebuhr describes this aesthetic logic which attempts to locate particular actions in a larger meaningful pattern.

We seek to have them fit into the whole as a sentence fits into a paragraph in a book, a note into a chord in a movement in a symphony, as the act of eating a common meal fits into the lifelong companionship of a family, as the decision of a statesman fits into the ongoing movement of his nation's life with other nations, or as the discovery of a scientific artifact fits into the history of science.[21]

The personal history of the individual and of the believing community, therefore, can shape the process of discernment so that this sense of self can be a trustworthy criterion for decision. The self as an emerging character in time and society is a more adequate criterion for serious decisions than any religious experience which prescinds from the story of the individual or of the believing community.[22]

The second major way in which symbols guide the reasoning heart of discernment is through interpreting events to unearth their religious significance. After considering the general pattern of symbolic interpretation of events, we will apply this reflection to the specific situation of the nuclear threat.

Discernment seeks the disclosure of the whole in the part. This movement complements that in which the individual part is illuminated by its context. As David Tracy notes, the claim which religion makes to truth is a disclosure of the whole, a revelatory model of meaning. "Unlike the classics of art, morality, science and politics, explicitly religious classic expressions will involve a claim to truth as the event of a disclosure-concealment of the whole of reality *by the power of the whole—*

---

[20] "I would only add that scripture creates more than a world; it shapes a community which is the bearer of that world. Without that community, claims about the moral authority of scripture—or rather the very idea of scripture itself—make no sense. Furthermore, I shall argue that claims about the authority of scripture make sense only in that the world and the community it creates are in fact true to the character of God" (ibid. 55).

[21] Niebuhr, *Responsible Self* 97.

[22] Although Rahner appreciates the gradual self-definition which occurs over time, he does not develop any account of moral character as it bears on present experience.

as, in some sense, a radical and finally gracious mystery."[23] Symbols are the appropriate vehicles of disclosure. They are the prisms which refract experience in novel ways for the imagination.

Religious discernment uses symbols to seek the disclosure of the gracious mystery of God in social events as well as personal ones. It seeks to discover more than God's call as a specific invitation to action. In the public realm it searches for the action of God challenging and redeeming in all events. The symbols and stories of Scripture function as paradigms for reading the signs of the times for the disclosure of God's action.

This disclosure of the whole in the part comes to the participant in faith, to the reasoning heart which looks for revelation and is willing to be instructed by it.[24] At first glance it seems that when we move from the question "Who am I?" to the question "What is going on?" we have left the standpoint of the participant for the standpoint of the objective observer. However, to answer that second question we necessarily refer to events, and there can be no single objective description of events which exhausts their meaning. To understand events, realities which occur in our experience, we need to complement the reasoning head with the reasoning heart. The discerning heart reasons by evaluating events from different angles and trying to fit them into different contexts.

Events cannot be dissected to find their causes. Their meaning is not readily available for public inspection, like the ingredients listed on the label of a can. For example, the events of Paul's ministry disclosed only a pattern of failure to his Gnostic opponents in Corinth. In the Second Letter to the Corinthians Paul interprets them in an entirely different context which discloses new meaning (1:8–10):

Brothers, we do not wish to leave you in the dark about the trouble we had in Asia: we were crushed beyond our strength, even to the point of despairing of life. We were left to feel like men condemned to death, so that we might trust not in ourselves but in God who raises from the dead. He rescued us from the

---

[23] David Tracy, *The Analogical Imagination* (New York: Crossroad, 1981) 163. "In an analogous fashion, religion, like art, discloses new resources of meaning and truth to anyone willing to risk allowing that disclosure to 'happen' " (ibid. 67).

[24] "What concerns us at this point is not the fact that the revelatory moment shines by its own light and is intelligible in itself but rather that it illuminates other events and enables us to understand them. Whatever else revelation means it does mean an event in our history which brings rationality and wholeness into the confused joys and sorrows of personal existence and allows us to discern order in the brawl of communal histories. Such revelation is no substitute for reason; the illumination it supplies does not excuse the mind from labor; but it does give to that mind the impulsion and the first principles it requires if it is to be able to do its proper work" (H. Richard Niebuhr, *The Meaning of Revelation* [New York: Macmillan, 1941] 80). Much of what is contained in this article on the reasoning heart is derivative from this masterly work.

danger of death and will continue to do so.[25]

Paul reverses the very charges of his detractors: his sufferings are rather the actual credentials for his ministry than proof of its failure. "Therefore I am content with weakness, with mistreatment, with distress, with persecutions and difficulties for the sake of Christ; for when I am powerless, it is then that I am strong" (12:10). When interpreted in the light of Christ's death and resurrection, these same facts come to bear a very different meaning. God's action is disclosed and that calls for an appropriate response.

In the middle of the Second World War, Niebuhr performed one of these symbolic interpretations of public events. He tried to interpret, or make sense out of, the suffering of innocent victims of war by asking the question "What is God doing in the war?" He employed the biblical symbols of divine judgment and the crucifixion in this interpretation. From viewing the war through these new lenses, he concluded that God was on neither side in the war and was judging all parties for their self-interest and self-righteousness. The scandal of innocent suffering of millions who were caught between the great armies could be meaningful only when seen in the context of Jesus Christ's vicarious suffering.[26]

Niebuhr's question offended nearly as many of his readers as did his answers. "What is God doing in the war?" grated on the sensibilities of those who protested that the benevolent Father of all could only grieve over human sinfulness in war. Niebuhr insisted that God must be doing something in every event, even in the most tragic. Either we are monotheists who are disposed to look for the presence of the one sovereign Lord in every deed and suffering, or we will be polytheists who assign portions of reality to another deity. Nevertheless, God is not the Great Manipulator of the universe who predetermines every action. Jesus believed that "the will of God is what God does in all that nature and man do. . . . The Universal One whom he calls Father is Lord of heaven and earth. His action is more like that of the great wise leader who uses even the meannesses of his subjects to promote the general welfare."[27] To be truly responsible in faith, Christians need to imitate Jesus in seeking out the hidden divine intention by locating even destructive events in the context of God's creating, redeeming, and judging activity.

What if we ask this strange question today: "What is *God* doing in the global buildup of armaments and the threat of nuclear annihilation?" If

---

[25] This and subsequent scriptural texts are from *The New American Bible* (Nashville: Thomas Nelson, 1971).

[26] H. Richard Niebuhr, "War as the Judgment of God," *Christian Century* 59 (1942) 630–33; "War as Crucifixion," ibid. 60 (1943) 513–15.

[27] Niebuhr, *Responsible Self* 164–65.

we restrict our discussion to the judgments of rationality employed in just-war reasoning, this fundamental question cannot even be raised. Using certain biblical symbols as lenses, we can attempt to discover an appropriate response to the signs of the times. The black civil-rights movement and Latin American liberation theology encourage this interpretation. Both movements read the situation of oppression through the lens of the Exodus symbol, and this has given direction in faith to millions in their struggle for justice.

Which symbols should we use? Scripture contains a wide range of symbolic events; hence selecting the appropriate ones must be done critically. The reasoning head must establish some general criteria for using biblical symbols. Since judgments of affectivity presuppose moral judgments of rationality as outer limits of action, this symbolic interpretation should be consonant with sound moral reasoning. The appropriate symbols must be central to the overall message of the canon. They should correlate with an image of God which coheres with the full teaching of the Scriptures. If taken from the Old Testament, these symbols must be consistent with the fundamental event of God's definitive revelation in Jesus Christ. The Exodus from Egypt is central to Israel's faith consciousness, correlates with the basic image of God as Redeemer, and foreshadows the cross and resurrection. Whether it leads to morally sound judgments must be determined from the particular application.

On the other hand, an inadequate symbol will function as "an evil imagination of the heart" which will disclose only a self-serving meaning and distort the truth of who we are and what we are doing.[28] The Dutch Calvinists of South Africa are accustomed to justify apartheid by appealing to their national election and the canonically minor symbol of "taking the Land" from the Canaanites. This symbol also fails the test of adequacy to the New Testament and leads to conclusions that violate ordinary moral standards.

One set of biblical symbols already operates in some thinking on the nuclear issue: that of crusade and martyrdom. An alternative symbol, which may yield a more illuminating significance for faith, is that of Israel's exile in Babylon.

Part of the legacy of the Cold War which affects the nuclear issue are the images of martyrdom and crusade which shaped Cold War rhetoric. The communist challenge was not fundamentally ideological but religious. An atheistic and monolithic totalitarian state threatened our way of life and religious liberty. This interpretation pointed to two responses.

---

[28] "Evil imaginations in this realm are shown to be evil by their consequences to selves and communities just as erroneous concepts and hypotheses in external knowledge are shown to be fallacious by their results" (Niebuhr, *Meaning of Revelation* 73).

Passively, one would prefer to endure martyrdom rather than give up the Christian faith. This symbol proved to be helpful as it guided the resistance of Christians to religious persecution in Eastern Europe and China. In a more active mode this vision employed the image of the crusade to marshal defenses. War becomes holy when waged for God's cause; the rhetoric of John Foster Dulles and others underlined the godless character of communism to prepare an arsenal of nuclear and conventional weaponry.

Despite some attempts to justify the crusade symbol from the Old Testament, it appears to be an evil imagination of the heart. Roland H. Bainton traces the crusade mentality back to the holy war of Judges and Deuteronomy. It renders an image of a God who delights in battle and exterminates the enemy without distinction of guilt or innocence. When Europe was threatened by the forces of Islam, the crusaders tended to ignore the restraints on knightly warfare. Bainton describes how the Allied cause in the Second World War was corrupted by becoming a crusade:

The enemy being beyond the pale, the code of humanity collapses. . . .Those who have fought in a frenzy of righteousness against the enemies of God—or of the democratic way of life—are disposed to demand unconditional surrender, thus prolonging resistance by their refusal to state terms. The crusader is severely tempted to arbitrariness in the final settlement, for the mood of holiness leads to the punishment of war criminals by the victors under the fictitious trappings of impartial justice.[29]

A truly evil imagination of the heart occurs when we merge the symbols of martyrdom and godly crusade in the nuclear era. Then it appears better to destroy the infidel even at the cost of our own lives. However, martyrdom which takes the whole world into its blessed sacrifice becomes demonic. Martyrdom connotes self-sacrifice, not the wilful sacrifice of countless others. Murder-suicide would be a more truthful symbol for nuclear vengeance.

What would be a more adequate symbol for interpreting the nuclear threat? It would have to be more appropriate to the contemporary situation than to Cold War realities. It would also have to indicate a more authentic faith response than crusade or martyrdom. The exile of the Israelites in Babylon may help to revision the nuclear issue. After being conquered by the Babylonians and subjected to mass deportation, Israel faced a profound crisis of faith. If Marduk, the deity of their conquerors, had prevailed over Yahweh, then perhaps the God of Abraham was only a minor deity. The seventy years of exile deepened this

---

[29] Roland H. Bainton, *Christian Attitudes toward War and Peace* (Nashville: Abingdon, 1960) 243.

crisis. Since all the promises had come to nothing—the Temple, the Davidic monarchy, the Land—could this mean that the covenant was null and void?

Ironically, Israel broke through to a new kind of faith during the Exile. The prophets returned to their deepest faith memories to recognize that the Exile was a second Exodus, disclosing a purified image of God. Yahweh was not the warrior king who fought on the side of the righteous, nor the god of royal civil religion who propped up a specific way of life. In Babylon, Israel came to realize for the first time that Yahweh alone was God and sovereign over all the nations. God would still be God even if Israel were dominated by foreign enemies. Yahweh would deliver His people in His own time and re-establish the covenant with a newly repentant people.

Looking at our contemporary situation through the lens of the Exile discloses some common features, even though it does not dictate a single strategy of response. It can uncover at the root of our national defensiveness a fear of being dominated by communism, a fear which is nearly ultimate. God's cause is not identical with any nation's aspirations, and the loss of our wealth and freedom would not mean the end of God. Perhaps such a loss would enable us to discover the true God we had not known before. On the other hand, any nation which would willingly devastate God's creation rather than endure an exile thereby indicates that its ultimate allegiance is to a life of national affluence. If a symbolic discernment of national values issues in a call to repentance, that does not settle all the moral questions. Moral analysis through judgments of rationality and reformulation of policy through political prudence must complement a symbolic reinterpretation. Failure to attend to these dominant symbols can only escalate the danger that evil imaginations of the heart will guide our political strategy and moral debates.

Discernment remains a personal search for the action of God in one's own history and in the events of the world. Although its conclusions are not morally generalizable as judgments of rationality are, the reasoning heart of the Christian finds normative guidance in the symbols and story of revelation.

AFFECTIVE CRITERIA FOR DISCERNMENT

Christian discernment has a second set of criteria for discovering an adequate response to God: a specific set of affections which flow from the story of Jesus. These affections complement the symbols which seek the disclosure of God's intentions in events. They set a normative matrix which guides the *manner* of action, because the morality of an action is established by both what we do and how we do it. How we act should be appropriate to the distinctive values displayed in the biblical narrative.

These affections are not transitory feelings or unfathomable moods; they are deep convictions of the reasoning heart which dispose the moral agent to act in definite ways. Religious affections are virtues, since they are habits which dispose the agent to moral action with ease and delight; this traditional Puritan term emphasizes their felt quality in experience. Roman Catholic moral theology has followed Thomas Aquinas in giving the virtues a considerable role in moral decision-making. However, the narrative of the gospel did not enter into his definition of the virtues— that rested on an assumed common human nature, even though these natural virtues were elevated by the gift of charity. An American approach to discernment makes a more integral connection between the affections (or virtues) of the Christian life and the biblical narrative. The story of Israel and of Jesus can thereby provide both symbols and a distinctive set of affections as criteria for discernment.

Karl Rahner's account of discernment discounts any role for a distinctive set of affections for two reasons. First, Rahner has no developed theory of human affectivity. Because the core of the person is self-defining freedom before God, felt dispositions are only the raw material on which freedom operates. Their moral significance arises only when they are caught up in the movement of human transcendence; he does not discuss their positive role in disposing the moral agent to evaluate and act.[30]

In addition, Rahner assigns the Gospels a minimal role in shaping the content of Christian ethics. He distinguishes a formal from a material dimension in the following of Christ, which reduces the contribution that Scripture can make to morality. The formal dimension is the same for all: a radical surrender to God made by explicit believers as well as those who are affected by grace "anonymously." "Once a man has reached Jesus, then it contains this simple message: just to be prepared to make the final act of hope and self-surrender to the incomprehensible mystery."[31] Formally, this self-surrender corresponds to the self-emptying of Jesus in the Incarnation and the cross. However, the actual conduct of the moral life, the material dimension, cannot be a copy of the life of Jesus. "The continuation of the life of Jesus that is new and different for each of us must be discovered by each individual in the way that is

---

[30] "If one were able to develop a theology and philosophy of freedom, it would become clear that freedom constitutes the very essence of emotion in comparison with which all other emotional factors would appear derivative, being mere conditions of possibility, a sign of the finite and passive character of created freedom and in the end analysable in terms of freedom" (Rahner, *TI* 16 [New York: Seabury, 1979] 64).

[31] Karl Rahner, *TI* 16, 18.

valid for him."[32] The love command does not refer to the specific historical example of Jesus; love resists definition, because it demands the person totally, not only in particular actions.[33]

When the natural law is the principle for interpreting the gospel, a certain leveling effect may inevitably occur. To maintain a moral system that is intelligible to those outside the Christian tradition, that tradition's distinctive contributions to reformulating moral standards and values is downplayed. In discernment a person asks not only about the morality of the action ("Is it right or wrong?") but also about the appropriateness of the action ("What kind of person does this sort of thing? Is it consistent with the person I am or want to be?"). To answer these questions, the Christian must turn to the central personal qualities which the biblical narrative exemplifies.

The American theological tradition has its roots in the Puritan experiment and in its ablest spokesman, Jonathan Edwards. In defending the conversion phenomena of the seventeenth-century Great Awakening, Edwards argued that sound religious affections are the true test of religious experience. His thesis was that "true religion, in great part, consists in holy affections."[34] In his masterpiece, *Religious Affections*, this Puritan pastor analyzed Christian conversion and growth as primarily a change of heart centering on the affections, the "springs that set men agoing, in all the affairs of life."[35] He provides twelve signs, culminating in consistent moral practice, by which the individual can gauge whether this change of heart has in fact occurred. Underlying them all as the primary gift of true conversion is a new capacity to appreciate the loveliness of God for its own sake. This same gift enables the convert to appreciate the credibility of sound doctrine and relish the goodness of proper conduct.

---

[32] Karl Rahner, *Spiritual Exercises* (New York: Herder and Herder, 1965) 119. Rahner's formal language about discernment does not do full justice to the practice of the Exercises. The retreatant only makes the "election," or serious life choice, after a lengthy period of meditating on the events of Jesus' life. He or she enters imaginatively into these scenes and uses the senses to appreciate them for days and even weeks. This consititutes a "school of the affections" which sets an aesthetic context to evaluate the decisions to be faced. Even more astonishing is the fact that in the eighty-six pages of the chapter of *Dynamic Element* on Ignatian discernment the name of Jesus Christ occurs only four times, and even these are only passing references. This appears a significant omission in analyzing Christian discernment as well as the Spiritual Exercises.

[33] See Karl Rahner, "The 'Commandment' of Love in Relation to the Other Commandments," *TI* 5 (Baltimore: Helicon, 1966) 456.

[34] Jonathan Edwards, *Religious Affections*, in John E. Smith, ed., *The Works of Jonathan Edwards* 2 (New Haven: Yale Univ., 1959) 95.

[35] Ibid. 101.

Authentic conversion produces a character which bears some resemblance to the character of Jesus depicted in the Gospels. The Holy Spirit gradually develops a specific set or constellation of affections in the Christian. These affections are the main dispositions which shape the person's character. This configuration of affections has a specific historical referent. Edwards held that one of the distinguishing signs of Christian affections is that "they naturally beget and promote such a spirit of love, meekness, quietness, forgiveness and mercy, as appeared in Christ."[36] Just as Paul could specify the fruits of the Spirit which he expected the Galatians to manifest, Edwards presumed that certain common traits would emerge in the diverse personalities of Christians. These affections correlate with the dispositions manifest by God and Christ in the work of redemption. "There is grace in Christians answering to grace in Christ, such an answerableness as there is between the wax and the seal; there is character for character: such kinds of graces, such a spirit and temper, the same things that belong to Christ's character, belong to theirs."[37]

While this is an ethics of the imitation of Christ, it is not primarily concerned with reproducing the external aspects of his life and work. Rather, those dispositions which were the main ingredients of the character of the Redeemer shape the character of the redeemed. As they grow in sanctification, mature Christians should come to prefer spontaneously the conduct which is consistent with the goodness of Christ.[38]

Why should there be a *specific* set of affections which characterize the Christian? Our affections are constituted by the objects toward which they tend. Because our faith holds certain things to be true about God and the world, affections which correspond to these convictions are evoked in our hearts. "The particularity of Christian affections has to do with the objects towards which they are directed," Don Saliers writes. "They are given their particular character by virtue of the stories, concepts and practices which belong to Christianity....To believe that God redeems, judges, and shows compassion for the contrite, involves a

---

[36] Ibid. 345.

[37] Ibid. 347.

[38] "That which men love, they desire to have and to be united to, and possessed of. That beauty which men delight in, they desire to be adorned with. Those acts which men delight in, they necessarily incline to do" (ibid. 394). Edwards' Christian ethics is a sustained response to the British "moral sense" philosophers, particularly Hutcheson and Shaftesbury. Against their position, he insisted that only the gift of the Holy Spirit could enable such a moral sense to function consistently and through trials. See Norman Fiering, *Jonathan Edwards' Moral Thought and Its British Context* (Chapel Hill: Univ. of North Carolina, 1981).

distinctive set of affections."[39] Dispositions and beliefs are mutually interdependent, because the belief shapes the affection and the affection enlivens and illumines the belief. Could one know the meaning of God's mercy without personally experiencing forgiveness? On the other hand, the forgiven person needs to know the necessity of repentance and the possibility of hope if it is to be genuine Christian forgiveness. We move from one pole to the other: we can examine affections to see what their objects are, and we can examine the convictions of belief to determine what the appropriate affections should be.[40]

Because of this interdependence of affection and faith convictions, narrative and doxology are the most common ways in which the biblical authors confess their faith. Both literary forms involve the listener or speaker insofar as they evoke the affective response which is integral to their cognitive content. They also challenge the hearer to become a participant, to act in correspondence with the movement of the story of the confession. So the prophet praises Yahweh in Isaiah 40 with images which also pointedly address the despairing exiles in Babylon: "The Lord is the eternal God, creator of the ends of the earth. He does not faint nor grow weary. . . . He gives strength to the fainting; for the weak he makes vigor abound . . . they that hope in the Lord will renew their strength, they will soar as with eagles' wings; they will run and not grow weary, walk and not grow faint" (40:28–31). In doxology the memory of the faith community becomes a paradigm for action and for affection. The Psalms, for instance, repeatedly recall God's action in the Exodus to evoke the particular form of trust which correlates with the image of God as redeemer of the enslaved. Confession of faith involves the whole person, as the reasoning heart illumines the path from conviction to action through engaging the appropriate affections.

[39] Don E. Saliers, *The Soul in Paraphrase* (New York: Seabury, 1980) 12, 19. "The essential feature of the order among Christian emotions is that they take God and God's acts as their object and ground" (ibid. 12).

[40] The object and its appropriate affection are so interrelated that the convictions of faith are not mere speculative knowledge but are "sensible knowledge." "That sort of knowledge by which a man has a sensible perception of amiableness and loathsomeness, or of sweetness and nauseousness, is not just the same sort of knowledge with that, by which he knows what a triangle is and what a square is. The one is mere speculative knowledge; the other sensible knowledge, in which more than the mere intellect is concerned; the heart is the proper subject of it, or the soul as a being that not only beholds, but has inclination, and is pleased or displeased. And yet there is the nature of instruction in it; as he that has perceived the sweet taste of honey, knows much more about it, than he who has only looked upon and felt it" (Edwards, *Religious Affections* 272). Sensible knowledge is one form of judgments of affectivity. Note the resemblance to Newman's distinction between real and notional assent: John Henry Newman, *A Grammar of Assent* (New York: Doubleday, 1955) chap. 4.

The biblical narratives enter into the definition of Christian affections because they embody the meaning of the affections metaphorically. Hauerwas writes that all virtues are narrative-dependent because their meaning is inseparable from a way of life. Only the story of an individual or a people can display how the qualities it endorses should become realized in our lives. Christian virtues are distinctive because the narrative on which they depend is the story of Jesus Christ.[41] Christian convictions do not merely provide additional motivation to enact natural virtuous dispositions; they also redefine these dispositions. "The singular feature of Christian rejoicing is that it occurs even in the midst of suffering, pain, and tribulation—even in the midst of grief.... The language which describes the world as God's creation and the arena of divine mercy is related *internally* to the ability to rejoice in all circumstances—even in the midst of suffering."[42]

Although this configuration of specific Christian dispositions is inseparable from the story of Jesus, some summary of them is possible. James Gustafson refers to these dispositions as "senses of the heart" which are the main threads in the fabric of Christian life: a sense of radical dependence, of gratitude, repentance, obligation, possibility, and direction. These dispositions are mutually sustaining and interdependent: repentance which lacks a sense of possibility and hope would not be faithful to the biblical witness. Together they provide the Christian with a set of reasons for being moral and serve as intentions to act in specific ways. Hence they ground a "moral life of a qualitatively different sort."[43] Gustafson bases these reasons for being moral on the particular images of God which are displayed in biblical revelation and confirmed in the present experience of believers.

These distinctive Christian affections can serve to discern appropriate action in two ways. First, they set an affective matrix against which options are gauged to see if they are harmonious or not. This affective

---

[41] Hauerwas argues that no universal account of human virtue can be given since the virtues are distinctively ordered and defined by the traditions which form them. While I agree with the penetration of virtue by a narrative tradition, I believe that some general descriptions of specific virtues can have cross-cultural intelligibility. Judgments of rationality are possible about virtues, even if they fall short of the description of character necessary to embody these skills. See Hauerwas, *Truthfulness and Tragedy* (Notre Dame: Univ. of Notre Dame, 1977) chaps. 3 and 4.

[42] Saliers, *Soul in Paraphrase* 66.

[43] James M. Gustafson, *Can Ethics Be Christian?* (Chicago: Univ. of Chicago, 1975) 92. "How one lives morally is related to these senses, and their accompanying tendencies in a moral direction, not only in terms of what persons and communities do, but also in terms of their perspectives on life, their perceptions of what is morally significant about events, their deliberations and their motivations" (ibid. 94). See also Gustafson, *Ethics from a Theocentric Perspective* 1 (Chicago: Univ. of Chicago, 1981) 197–204.

matrix corresponds to the qualities manifest in the Gospel story. The Christian "tests the spirits to see if among all the forces that move within him, his societies, the human mind itself, there is a uniting, a knowing, a whole-making spirit, a Holy Spirit. And he can do so only with the aid of the image, the symbol of Christ. 'Is there a Christ-like spirit there?' "[44] Niebuhr has brought together here the central resources of the reasoning heart in discernment: symbol and affectivity as they mutually define each other and form an aesthetic test of action.

As the Christian affections become deeply rooted in the character through practice responsive to God's call, they can intuitively suggest appropriate behavior. Edwards noted that mature Christians often come to decisions without "a long chain of reasoning," by means of a certain discerning taste. Just as a well-trained palate detects what is missing in a sauce, so the relish for the divine beauty can inform a mature Christian how to act.

Yea its holy taste and appetite leads it to think of that which is truly lovely, and naturally suggests the idea of its proper object . . . whereby, in the lively exercise of grace, [a holy person] easily distinguishes good and evil, and knows at once, what is a suitable amiable behavior towards God, and towards man, in this case and the other; and judges what is right, as it were spontaneously, and of himself, without a particular deduction, by any other arguments than the beauty that is seen and goodness that is tasted.[45]

Edwards recognizes how dispositions guide moral intuition, the knowledge by "connaturality" familiar to Catholic moral theology.[46] Yet Edwards is no intuitionist: these intuitions must be conformable to both the rules and the dispositions presented in the gospel. In our terms, judgments of affectivity complement without contravening the judgments of rationality in moral reflection.[47]

Rahner also uses affectivity as a criterion for discernment but makes it only formally dependent upon the biblical narrative. In commenting on Loyola's Exercises he notes a sense of radical peace and openness to God which tests the authenticity of possible inspirations. However, he

---

[44] Niebuhr, *Responsible Self* 155.

[45] Edwards, *Religious Affections* 282. Edwards' admission of this spontaneous awareness of what is to be done is surprising, given his consistent suspicion of "enthusiasm" or direct divine inspiration of particular content.

[46] "Any singular moral judgment is a judgment by way of inclination and it will be a good one if I am inclined to what is my true good" (Ralph McInerny, "Maritain and Poetic Knowledge," *Renascence* 34 [1982] 207). The proviso is crucial, because the vicious person will have knowledge which is affectively connatural to the vicious principles that dominate his or her character.

[47] See Edwards, *Religious Affections* 387, on the necessary convergence between the affections and the moral standards of the gospel.

centers almost exclusively on surrender to the absolute mystery of God as the affective touchstone.[48] Because they attend to the diverse images of God and the particularities of the story of Jesus, American theologians are able to make a richer purchase of biblical material for an affective matrix for discernment. If there is any formal pattern running through biblical ethics, it finds expression in the new commandment of Jesus in Jn 13:34: "Love one another just as I have loved you." This formal principle refers the believer immediately back to the "material," the memory of the actual ways in which Jesus Christ loved. These memories have some correspondence in the experience of the Christian, and they can set a diverse matrix for affective testing of discernment. In sum, Christians are called to be human in a specific way, not through copying an ancient portrait but in having different reasons of the heart for being moral.

Christian discernment brings to light rich elements in moral decision-making. Judgments of affectivity legitimately ground some moral decisions through the discriminating functions of memory and imagination. These judgments are evaluated not by formal logic but by aesthetic criteria: by the sense of self, the evaluation of events through biblical symbols, and the correlation between certain ways of acting and the configuration of Christian affections. Because these criteria are normative within the public tradition of the Christian community, discernment is not finally accountable only to itself. The classic authors of Christian spirituality such as Jonathan Edwards and Ignatius Loyola have long realized the importance of discernment in Christian practice. Contemporary American theologians have a significant contribution to make to Catholic moral theology in critically integrating discernment into Christian ethics.

These same theologians can broaden the common Roman Catholic notion of discernment. Not only can we look for God's gracious disclosure in specific invitations but also in integrating our own histories and reading the signs of the times. Their rationale presents the hope that those who find God in some things may eventually be led to find God in all things.

---

[48] Rahner, *Dynamic Element* 154. Although he analyzes with his usual care the words of Ignatius to describe the affections of that "consolation" which is the sign of the Spirit, he fails to attend to the fuller matrix of affective criteria which the previous meditations on the life of Christ have established. Not only the goals of one's aspirations need to be in harmony with these dispositions, but also the means which one proposes to use to attain these goals. Since we rarely reach our goals, our lives become morally stamped by the means we live with. The means need to justify our ends.

John R. Stacer

Divine Reverence for Us: God's Being Present, Cherishing, and Persuading

John R. Stacer, S.J., teaches philosophy at Loyola University, New Orleans. His chief interests are ethics, the philosophy of God, and American philosophy, in particular, the thought of William E. Hocking, Alfred North Whitehead and William James.

IN THE SPIRIT of our United States Founding Fathers, we live in a tradition of reverence for human dignity. Our respect for the life and freedom of every human person is grounded in a conviction that in this regard all are created equal. As our national community became aware of slavery's irreverence, slavery was abolished. As we became aware that denying the vote and forcing segregation were irreverent, these evils were largely overcome. Frequently those who challenged irreverence did so in the name of God, who has reverence for all human persons and invites us to have an analogous reverence.

In recent years, however, we have become aware of irreverence growing in our world: violent crime, death of the handicapped, abortion, starvation, torture, threat of nuclear war. Rightly we feel pangs of discontent at this irreverence. How can we challenge it? What are its roots? Three roots of irreverence are a failure to be realistically present to those who suffer, a failure to cherish all persons, and a failure to persuade others rather than coerce them.

A failure to be realistically present to those who suffer is evidenced by the phenomenon of psychic numbing. Robert Jay Lifton has studied this deadening of awareness in survivors of Hiroshima and in workers who produce nuclear bombs and missiles.[1] Hiroshima survivors tell others that they were out of town when the bomb exploded, and some think it themselves despite physiological and psychological evidence to the contrary. The reality is too evil to face. Analogously, arms producers and deployers refuse to talk about missiles or weapons, only "vehicles" or "delivery systems." For them there come to be no bombs or warheads, only "devices" or "nose cones." The cover-up of psychic numbing is directly irreverent toward the human right to truth and the natural human knowing process; it may also be used as a cultivated and invalid excuse for further irreverence against human life and freedom.

[1] *Death in Life: Survivors of Hiroshima* (New York: Random House, 1968).

77

A failure to cherish all persons is evidenced by the fact that some in the United States lack effective respect for life—life of the handicapped, of the unborn, of those who starve to death because global resources go to the arms race. A great variety of researchers state that starvation could be eliminated if between 5% and 10% of the global arms budget were devoted to the fight against hunger.[2] As early as 1976 the Holy See's Statement to the United Nations put the truth strongly: "The arms race is to be condemned unreservedly. . . . [It is] *in itself an act of aggression* against those who are the victims of it. It is an act of aggression which amounts to a crime, for *even when they are not used,* by their cost alone *armaments kill the poor by causing them to starve.*"[3] Were we free from psychic numbing or cover-up, we would name the arms race what it is: objective mass murder, a serious irreverence against human life.

A failure to persuade and a lapse into coercion is evidenced by our nation's threatening others with arms rather than inviting others with wise diplomacy and with farsighted and foresighted economic policies. Those who control the First and Second Worlds think they are threatened, so they threaten, are threatened in return, and so on in a vicious spiral. Moreover, our "national security" mentality brings torture as well as starvation to the Third World. Dom Helder Câmara challenges us "to continue to demand an end to torture, but we must discover the roots of torture. These roots lie in the absolutization of 'national security.' This ideology came from the United States to the high-level military schools in Latin America."[4] Were we free from psychic numbing or cover-up, we would name the national-security mentality what it is: objective support of torture, a serious irreverence against human freedom.

The religious person can challenge these three roots by recalling that God made us in His image and likeness. God is reverent toward us, and God invites us to be analogously reverent toward one another. Since our irreverence is rooted in a lack of presence, of cherishing, and of persuasion, we may be helped by centering on a God who is reverently present to us, who cherishes us, who persuades us and does not coerce. Such divine reverence for us is the focus of the present chapter's three main sections. They are preceded by a section on a method which incorporates reverence for the rich subjectivity of the human knower and for the multifaceted character of the object known.

[2] See Michael T. Klare, "The Global Arms Trade," and Patrice Franko, "Swords into Plowshares: Demilitarizing Development Strategies," *New Catholic World* 226, no. 1346 (March–April 1982) 64–67 and 74–77.

[3] "Statement of the Holy See to the United Nations (1976)," in *A Race to Nowhere: An Arms Race Primer for Catholics* (Chicago: Pax Christi, U.S.A.) 44. All emphasis within texts cited in this article is that of the original authors.

[4] Joseph E. Mulligan, "The United States and Brazil: An Interview with Dom Helder Câmara," *America* 141, no. 10 (Oct. 13, 1979) 194.

Philosophy is my professional field, and within it I focus mainly on the philosophy of God. The two thinkers who help me most are William Ernest Hocking (1873–1966) and Alfred North Whitehead (1861–1947). Hocking centered on religious experience, bringing together the best from his teachers William James and Josiah Royce. Whitehead constructed the original system around which the tradition of North American process philosophy and theology has grown. Since we three are philosophers, we begin our reflections from human experience—that experience taken whole. We would lack wholeness if we excluded from our data faith experience or its expression, including its expression in Scripture. Hocking and Whitehead are free to quote Scripture—not as proof texts but as reports of human experience—and I am free to quote them quoting Scripture. Yet we do philosophy of God and not theology.

The distinctive contribution of this article is that it sketches a philosophy of divine reverence for us. Since our method includes reverent musement, whole-aspect alternation, and mystic-prophet alternation, these receive brief attention in an initial section. Since the divine reverence for us is expressed in God's being present, cherishing, and persuading, these three aspects of the divine life are the foci of the article's three main sections. Hocking and Whitehead help me develop all these points, but in the chapter their reflections are subordinate to mine. The strong focus on divine reverence and the organization of thought to develop the notion of reverence are my contribution.

HUMAN REVERENCE IN METHOD: MUSEMENT AND ALTERNATION

A method appropriate for a philosophical approach to God's reverence for us is analogous to a way of developing a friendship. At times it is informal; it both takes in the whole picture and centers on details; it involves give-and-take.

Musement is a first important aspect of our method, an aspect first developed by Charles Sanders Peirce and further developed by Josiah Royce, then by Hocking, Whitehead, and others. It is a way of gradually coming to an insight and then confirming it, without relying mainly on clear mathematical intuition or formal logical demonstration. We cannot simply look at a person and say "friend" the way we look at a mathematical figure and say "triangle." Nor can we give a logical demonstration that a person is a friend the way we demonstrate a geometrical theorem. There are hard and fast rules neither for developing a friendship nor for musement, but there are helps. We need to be with a person for some time to become friends; so we need to muse about a topic for some time in order gradually to see the light. In making friends we use imagination, and informally we catch loose analogies between a new friend and some old friend; so also musement is imaginative and uses analogies. About a friend-to-be we notice not merely facts but also values; we do not just understand, we feel attracted by beauty of character; so musement is open to value, to feeling, to beauty. Friends do not let themselves become trapped in excessive seriousness; so musement can be playful. Friends tell each other stories, true and make-believe; so musement uses narratives, be they history or myth or parable.

The last paragraph is itself an example of musement. I made no attempt to define it by genus and species. Rather, I offered an analogy between musement and developing a friendship, then touched informally on various aspects of the analogy to offer some insight into what musement is about. Nor did I try to prove that musement exists. Rather, I let myself experience some musement, told about it, and invited the reader to notice. Now religious experience is developing a friendship with God. It is only natural that musement should be of service to it.

In general, alternation is rhythmic shifting of attention which keeps human experiencing both realistic and alive. Hocking is the thinker who makes it most explicit, but it is present in Royce, Whitehead, and others.

Alternation between vision of a whole and centering on an aspect is a second important facet of our method. In getting to know a friend, we now size up the other as a whole, now zero in on some definite character trait. Then we back away to get the person more into perspective, follow by again centering on some particular. We feel the general thrust of the other's life, and single events also invite our attention. There is a similar whole-aspect alternation in our coming to know a community and its history. Now we take in the group as a whole and notice the networks of relationships, now we center on the character of a particular individual.

Whole-aspect alternation enables us to overcome both narrowness and vagueness, each in turn. It combats the overly analytic tendency of many thinkers since Hobbes and Descartes, the temptation to fragment reality by reifying what are only aspects of a unified whole—perhaps because this fabricates false security by psychically numbing us to other aspects which we do not control. It also combats the tendency to vagueness of thinkers who analyze too little and so fail to notice much.

Alternation between receiving and contributing is a third important aspect of our method. It is exemplified in the give-and-take of friends. Now one receives from the other, now he or she gives. A friendship will stagnate and die if either person does nothing but give or nothing but receive, nothing but challenge or nothing but appreciate. Each phase is meant to prepare for the next contrasting phase. As Hocking puts it in religious language, "the meaning of the mystic experience is prophetic."[5]

---

[5] *MG* 439. *MG* refers to Hocking, *The Meaning of God in Human Experience* (New Haven: Yale University, 1912).

An everyday mystic is any person who in a broad sense is receptive in prayer; an everyday prophet is any person who in a broad sense is productive of some lasting good effect.[6]

We are called to be mystics and prophets, each in its turn. "It is by the alternation of loyalty and worship that each life must hold and increase its individual level of value."[7] In mystical moments of worship we increase our value by being receptive to God's gift of renewed purpose. In prophetic moments of loyalty we hold our value by acting in accord with our gift; purpose not acted upon is weakened. Like others for whom religion naturally leads to ethics and vice versa, I find that to teach the philosophy of God invites me also to teach ethics and vice versa. My religious appreciation of God's reverence leads me to an ethical challenge confronting human irreverence such as arms production, and my ethics of human reverence leads me to a natural theology of divine reverence.

Mystic-prophet alternation is based on the fact that we should act in accord with who we are and who others are. Hocking recognizes that "the Christian code becomes possible, even imperative" when we perceive each human person as "having something of the divine in him—'ye have done it unto me'—hence worthy of reverence, 'even the least of these.' This the deeepest reach of the Christian ethic is an immediate consequence of the deepest reach of its world view, whereby each person participates in the life of God."[8] The Christian world view includes the recognition that God's reverence makes every person participate in divine life—at least in that, like God, we can know, love, and freely decide. As a consequence, each of us is invited to join God in reverencing every person, others or self. Accordingly, the divine reverence for us will be the chapter's central focus, a more mystical receptive focus; but at times we will employ alternation and shift to a more prophetic focus on the reverence we should have for one another.

GOD WHO IS REVERENTLY PRESENT

A first major characteristic of all reverence is not distance but presence. In some times and places formality has been or is a sign of reverence, since then and there it could facilitate presence. Yet formality is not necessarily connected with reverence; if it brings about distance, it is a problem. Normally, presence of an appropriate kind is a first sign of reverence, and we should not be surprised that it is a characteristic of divine reverence.

---

[6] Admittedly, this use of "prophet" is very analogous, but it can be justified by the fact that the everyday prophet "challenges" the inadequacy of a situation which was less good before his or her contribution than after.

[7] *MG* 439–40.

[8] *CWC* 94. *CWC* refers to Hocking, *The Coming World Civilization* (London: George Allen & Unwin, 1958).

The recent "death of God" theology denied God's presence. For it, God first lived as transcendent, then really emptied Himself in the Incarnation and really annihilated Himself in Christ's death. Thus "a radically profane history is the inevitable consummation of an actual movement of the sacred into the profane."[9] The "good news" is that we are no longer dominated by a transcendent absolute.

We never were thus dominated. "Death of God" theologians correctly challenged the man-made idol of a coercive absolute who would accord us no responsibility, who would give us no participation in the divine knowing and loving and deciding. But they were mistaken to challenge God's continuing existence and presence. With Hocking and Whitehead, I hold for a God who does not coerce us but does enliven us. We experience our best selves in the presence of such a God.

In my philosophy the first main characteristic of God's reverence for us is divine presence to us. I reflect on three aspects. God's presence sustains us, enlivening us and giving us purpose. God's presence supports our better selves, opening us to our responsibility and to reality as it is. God's presence may be directly verified in holistic experience; it invites our receptive attention and does not require proof.

God's presence sustains us, giving us life and purpose. As Hocking puts it, God is "experienced . . . as a creative will sustaining my own being (hence caring for my existence), an activity inviting a response."[10] In metaphysical terms, through efficient causation God sustains my being; through final causation God invites my response. The sustaining-inviting is one divine activity. In Whitehead's system God communicates creativity by establishing a free creature as most basically an aim, a purpose. God's power simultaneously sustains a free creature's existence and invites the creature's harmonious activity: "The power by which God sustains . . . is the power of himself as the ideal"[11] inviting our response. Such power is exercised with reverence; as we shall see more fully in the section on God's persuasion, it sustains us and invites us but does not coerce.

God's presence supports our better selves, opening us to our own responsibility and to reality as it is. Both zest and peace are signs of God's presence. "It is the immanence of the Great Fact including this initial Eros and this final Beauty which constitutes the zest of self-forgetful transcendence belonging to Civilization at its height."[12] The

[9] Thomas J. J. Altizer, *The Gospel of Christian Atheism* (Philadelphia: Westminster, 1966) 109.

[10] *MG* xiii (1963). In 1963 Hocking wrote an additional preface to the major work he had written fifty years earlier. References to the new preface add "1963" after the page number.

[11] *RM* 156. *RM* refers to Whitehead, *Religion in the Making* (New York: Macmillan, 1926).

[12] *AI* 381. *AI* refers to Whitehead, *Adventures of Ideas* (New York: Macmillan, 1933).

"Great Fact" refers to God; in Whitehead "immanence" does not imply pantheism but does refer to divine presence. As "initial Eros," God enlivens and invites us by giving us purpose; as "final Beauty," God cherishes our excellence. The divine inviting is immediately experienced in our zest. Trust in the harmony of the universe which God invites toward beauty makes possible our self-forgetful transcendence. In similar terms, Hocking finds that the experience of God's presence underlies our "*self-confidence*," our "*empirical openness*," and our sense of "*responsibility*."[13] Religion which appreciates God's enlivening presence is far from an opiate.

God's presence is directly verified in holistic experience; it invites our receptive attention and does not require proof. We can "directly verify" God's presence and existence.[14] We take part in an "encounter" with God, "the theme of the mystics of all ages."[15] We can all be everyday mystics who experience God in "*the forward thrust of being*, . . . felt but inarticulate. This never-assertive but never-absent metaphysical sense of process-and-direction to which all action trusts itself is, I dare say, the most primitive form of faith object; and our commitment thereto the dimmest version of natural religion."[16] We need not articulate what is never absent; it need not be subjected to analysis. Its nonassertiveness is a sign of God's reverence for our intelligence and freedom: God does not coerce our assent, as might a mathematical proposition; rather, God invites us to trust, as would a personal friend.

Now that our notion of divine presence has been sketched, we can understand better why "death of God" thinkers overlooked God's abiding presence. Since God is present sustaining my own life and inviting me, an overly analytic mode of thought might notice only self and not God. Thinkers influenced mainly by a European tradition from Hobbes and Descartes to Nietzsche are in danger of being trapped in analysis. Alternating from the analytic to the holistic mode, classic North Americans more easily notice the immediate experience of God's presence. It should be noted that a contemporary European such as Karl Rahner is sufficiently holistic and aware of God's presence. Thus, in his theology of grace Rahner stresses that grace is a gift of divine life which becomes intrinsic to us,[17] does respect our freedom and responsibility,[18] and is experienced by us.[19] I find Rahner more helpful in leading an overly analytic person step by step toward regaining wholeness. I find Hocking's

[13] *MG* 295–96.
[14] *MG* xi (1963).
[15] *MG* xii (1963).
[16] *CWC* 98.
[17] *Theological Investigations* 1 (Baltimore: Helicon, 1961) 302–10.
[18] *Grace in Freedom* (New York: Herder and Herder, 1969) 228–29.
[19] *Theological Investigations* 4 (Baltimore: Helicon, 1966) 178–84.

and Whitehead's inviting and imaginative expression more helpful in deepening a person's understanding of spontaneous holistic experience.

By now it should be clear that our reverent method for guiding human experience is a help toward being aware of God's reverent presence to us. We should not always demand proof; we should be open also to musement and direct experience of God's presence. We should not be trapped in analysis; we should be open also to holistic experience. We should not be caught in either the dropout of ceaseless contemplation or the burnout of driven action; we should alternate between a mystical prayer receptive to God's enlivening presence and a prophetic action loyal to a challenging aim given by God to each of us.

At the beginning of this section we saw that reverence requires neither formality nor distance; rather, it is characterized by presence. Another common misunderstanding is that the person revered must always be greater than the person revering. Yet God, who is the greatest, reveres each human person, reveres him as "having something of the divine in him—'ye have done it unto me'—hence worthy of reverence, 'even the least of these.'"[20] Our human reverence, too, is ultimately grounded not in individual varieties of human greatness but in what is true of the starving and tortured and of all men and women without exception: "each person participates in the life of God."[21] God is reverently present to each, sustaining life in the divine image and likeness.

GOD WHO REVERENTLY CHERISHES

A second major characteristic of all reverence is appreciative love: felt esteem for actualized value, particularly in persons. In scriptural accounts of religious experience, God cherishes us with feeling as would a mother, a father, a husband, or a brother. Yet Greek-influenced philosophy associated with God the problematic notion of "immutably perfect." As a result, some philosophers are of the opinion that God cannot experience a felt esteem for our good acts or a felt pain from our evil ones. Imagining that the perfect is changeless, they do not understand how we can make any difference to God. My position is that these philosophers consider God too abstractly and not holistically enough. They consider only the changeless divine core identity.

On the other hand, I distinguish between God's core identity and God's intentional consciousness, God's living operations of knowing, loving, and deciding. In this I agree with Whitehead that the "Divine Eros" includes more than a core of ideals; it includes also "the urge to their finite realization, each in its due season. Thus a process must be inherent

---

[20] *CWC* 94.   [21] *CWC* 94.

in God's nature, whereby His infinity is acquiring realization."[22] God's core identity is changeless; God cannot stop being God. Yet on the level of intentional consciousness—of knowing, loving, and freely deciding— it is more perfect (less limited) to experience living process than to be changeless. Immutability is a perfection only on the level of core identity. Immutability would be an imperfection on the level of living operations such as knowing, loving, and deciding.[23]

In my holistic philosophy the second main characteristic of divine reverence is God's cherishing us as persons. I reflect on four aspects. God's intentional consciousness is affected by what we do. God feels and remembers. When our acts are good, God feels delight and reinforces our delight. When our acts are evil, God shares our suffering, is not overcome by it, and encourages us not to be overcome.[24]

In intentional consciousness God is reverently receptive to us. Alternation is a characteristic of full and vibrant life. Should it not be an aspect of divine life as well as of human life? Such is our experience when we converse with God. Initially God speaks and we listen, then we speak and God listens. God's listening is an aspect of our holistic religious experience as Hocking recounts it: "For while God and Nature first become real to me because they determine me, they can only remain real, in so far as I also can successfully determine them, and as I intend."[25] When I freely affect another, I am not inclined to doubt the other's existence. Thus I experience God within the give-and-take of dialogue— of ethical discernment, of action, of prayer which is truly conversation. "I cannot passively find my friend as a ready-made friend"[26] applies also to friendship with God. The way in which I "make" God's intentional consciousness may be appreciated more fully through Whitehead's notion of a divine "Unity of Adventure." A first phase of this adventure is God's "Eros which is the living urge towards all possibilities," a loving invitation which urges us to grow and to relate. A second phase is God's "claiming the goodness of their realization"[27] as we actualize the possibilities. Our goodness and beauty are appreciated as contributions to the divine life. "This Beauty has always within it the renewal derived from the Advance

---

[22] AI 357.

[23] See my article "Integrating Thomistic and Whiteheadian Perspectives on God," International Philosophical Quarterly 21 (1981) 355-77.

[24] As we develop these aspects, it is particularly important to remember that our knowledge of God is always analogous. In these aspects God is different from us and not merely similar to us; our language falls far short of the divine reality. It should also be remembered that we center not on God's changeless core identity but on God's intentional consciousness, the living divine experience of knowing, loving, and deciding.

[25] MG 502.

[26] MG 140.

[27] AI 381.

of the Temporal World."[28] In the divine receptive phase God is renewed by our beauty, which God reverently cherishes.

God's receptivity is that "of a tenderness which loses nothing that can be saved."[29] Everlastingly God remembers our good. "The consequent nature of God is the fluent world become 'everlasting' by its objective immortality in God."[30] Since God does not forget, my deed achieves an immortality outside myself which satisfies the demands of a human "prophetic consciousness." For Hocking, this is not a present imagination of future actuality; it is a confidence that present action has a lasting effect. "It is an assurance of the future and of all time as determined by my own individual will, embodied in my present action."[31] Such an assurance is given in my low-keyed, holistic experience that one who does not forget is reverently receptive to me.

God feels delight in my good acts. There is no knowledge without an appropriate affective response, as Whitehead affirms by referring to all attentive experience as "feeling." God's feeling of esteem "is the mirror which discloses to every creature its own greatness."[32] Our human sense of worth is amplified by being mirrored back to us through the divine cherishing. One of Hocking's favorite Scripture texts, "Inasmuch as ye have done it unto one of the least of these my brethren, ye have done it unto me,"[33] suggests that God feels with delight the good we do for others and feels with pain the harm we do to them.

When we do wrong, God suffers from it but understands how the harm may be overcome. Whitehead uses the image "of the patience of God, tenderly saving the turmoil."[34] "God is the great companion, the fellow-sufferer who understands."[35] All-knowing, all-present, all-loving, God knows our human evil and the suffering it brings; God's affective response is the appropriate one, sympathy. With reverent patience, God does not overlook our suffering but shares it. Hocking recounts how we experience

---

[28] *AI* 381.

[29] *PR* 525. *PR* refers to Whitehead, *Process and Reality* (New York: Macmillan, 1929). Texts are cited as they appear in the Corrected Edition, ed. David Ray Griffin and Donald W. Sherburne (New York: Free Press, 1978). Pagination given is that of the original, available within brackets in the corrected edition and also available in other editions.

[30] *PR* 527. Whitehead makes no definitive statements for or against conscious personal immortality. Most interpreters agree with Charles Hartshorne in thinking that Whitehead's system tends toward its denial. In my December 1981 article in *International Philosophical Quarterly* I join those who hold that Whitehead's system tends toward the affirmation of conscious immortality. See especially Marjorie Suchocki, "The Question of Immortality," *Journal of Religion* 57 (1977) 298–302. Hocking consistently affirmed conscious immortality; he gave many sound philosophical reasons. See especially *The Meaning of Immortality in Human Experience* (New York: Harper, 1957).

[31] *MG* 503.

[32] *RM* 155.

[33] *CWC* 184.

[34] *PR* 525.

[35] *PR* 532.

the fact that God's suffering is redemptive: "*Association*. That pain which is taken in common, like effort which is carried on in common, is found through the association to lose its hardness."[36] Yet human association may cause destructive pain, may be terminated with the pain of loss, may be lacking in presence and knowledge. All-good, God is the only associate who cannot cause destructive pain. Eternal, God is the associate who most clearly cannot be lost. All-present and all-knowing, God is the perfect companion. Thus the burden of pain is best lifted by "God as intimate, infallible associate, present in all experience as That by Which I too may firmly conceive that experience from the outside. It is God in this personal relation ... that alone is capable of establishing human peace of mind, and thereby human happiness."[37] I can peacefully conceive the painful experience and not be overcome because God my companion experiences it and is not overcome. Thus the work of God's reverence is in part to promote human solidarity, "to render the individual more perfectly *open to experience*."[38] Such openness encourages the sympathy which invites me to work with God toward overcoming evil, as we will see in reflection on God's persuading.

Our musement on God's cherishing has been holistic. God creates freely, so no mere analysis of who God must be can arrive at God's cherishing us. Again, an overly analytic approach may block our experience of being cherished. Again, too, wholeness is being retrieved by contemporary European thinkers, particularly existentialists and phenomenologists. Gabriel Marcel wrote *Royce's Metaphysics*,[39] corresponded with Hocking, avowed the influence of Royce and Hocking with regard to his central notions of community and holistic experience. Marcel, in turn, was one influence on Pope John Paul II's notions of sympathy, participation, and solidarity. Intertwining influences connect Royce, Hocking, Marcel, Martin Buber, Edmund Husserl, Max Scheler, Karol Wojtyla, and others in their philosophies of community.[40] With this background we can better appreciate parts of Pope John Paul II's encyclical *On the Mercy of God*, parts which help us to experience God's felt esteem for our human dignity. We center on the parable of the prodigal son and on the crucifixion.

When the prodigal returns, the father's contagious merrymaking "indicates a good that has remained intact: even if he is a prodigal, a son

---

[36] *MG* 222.

[37] *MG* 224.

[38] *MG* 225.

[39] Chicago: Regnery, 1956.

[40] See especially Marcel, *Being and Having* (New York: Harper & Row, 1965); Scheler, *The Nature of Sympathy* (London: Routledge & Kegan Paul, 1954); Wojtyla, *The Acting Person* (Dordrecht, Holland: D. Reidel, 1979).

does not cease to be truly his father's son; it also indicates a good that has been found again, which in the case of the prodigal son was his return to the truth about himself."[41] Pope John Paul warns us that it would be a mistake to see in mercy a relationship of inequality such that "mercy belittles the receiver, that it offends the dignity of man." Rather, "the relationship of mercy is based on the common experience of that good which is man, on the common experience of the dignity which is proper to him."[42] Here is faithful cherishing, a divine reverence respectful of our abiding dignity as members of the divine family whether we return or we squander. Explicitly there is spontaneous "joyous emotion at the moment of the son's return home";[43] implicitly there is joy at all the son's good acts.

There is also felt pain at the son's squandering, which "could not be a matter of indifference to his father. It was bound to make him suffer."[44] Now when God suffers, He invites our mercy; thus mercy becomes reciprocal. "In a special way, God also reveals His mercy when He *invites men to have 'mercy' on His only Son, the crucified one.*"[45] Our free response should be one of loving compassion toward Christ, particularly as he is present in the hungry and the homeless: "As you did it to the least of these . . . you did it to me." Then our love "is not only an act of solidarity with the suffering Son of man, but also a kind of 'mercy' shown by each one of us to the Son of the eternal Father." In this "could man's dignity be more highly respected and ennobled, for, in obtaining mercy, He [Christ] is in a sense the one who at the same time 'shows mercy'?"[46] This "*disquieting model*" of "*Christ* crucified" emphasizes that "merciful love" ought to be "bilateral and reciprocal."[47] Pope John Paul's holistic philosophical notions of sympathy, participation, and solidarity shine through this challenging account of divine receptivity and reverent cherishing.

Mingled here are two somewhat different kinds of mercy. One is mercy for the sufferer—as for those who starve throughout the world because resources are squandered on arms. To feel this mercy, we need farsight, but with farsight sympathy comes spontaneously. Solidarity with "the least of these" requires mainly that we alternate out of narrow concerns

[41] Pope John Paul II, *On the Mercy of God* (1980) sect. 6, p. 22 in St. Paul ed.

[42] Ibid.

[43] Ibid., p. 21.

[44] Ibid., sect. 5, p. 20. In this context "father" need not represent the First Person of the Trinity. In context it is clear that God the Son suffers; there are no affirmations or implications regarding the Father.

[45] Ibid., sect. 8, p. 28.

[46] Ibid.

[47] Ibid., sect. 14, p. 42.

in order to envision the human community as a whole. Without too much difficulty we participate in God's reverently cherishing those who starve.

But how easily do we cherish those prodigals whose squandering causes the starvation? A second kind of mercy is for the seeming sinner—as for those whose "defense spending" we may feel murders the starving, prepares their own nuclear suicide, and treasonously plays the Marxist game by causing class struggle. It is not easy to be reverent toward those who seem irreverent, especially when they are not among the least but among the powerful. Here we may need conversion ourselves in order that we may alternate at times from a more prophetic stance of challenging the sin toward a more mystical stance of cherishing the sinner as a person, shift from a centered focus on distinct structures of oppression toward a broader holistic vision of the human community which embraces both the oppressed and the oppressor. For this conversion to happen, we need divine persuasion.

GOD WHO REVERENTLY PERSUADES

A third major characteristic of all reverence is an active respect for value which promotes value's actual realization. This involves a positive fostering of value, its preservation, not destroying it, and resistance to its destruction. With regard to human persons, the values of life and of freedom call for special respect. Promoting these values means renouncing destructive coercion in favor of reverent persuasion. The destructive coercion to be renounced includes war and the threat of war, subversion, torture, and economic oppression. The reverent persuasion to be favored means inviting free choice by truthful communication based on concern for the good of all, a good which includes meeting basic needs such as the need for food and education.

Recently freedom has been receiving special attention from Latin American theologies of liberation. The major affirmations of such theologies fit well with our philosophy of reverence: they call for our conversion and renew our sense of responsibility; they rightly challenge legalized irreverence and promote conscientization which alerts us to structural injustices; they oppose destructive coercion and seek the reconciliation of all. We in the United States should listen, for we can cease exporting the arms and the national-security mentality which fuel destructive violence. We can foster economic changes which allow people now oppressed to free themselves and meet their basic needs. Yet we may fail to enter sufficiently into the Third World perspective and thus miss the reverent persuasion with which the theologians seek "to liberate the oppressors from their own power, from their ambition, and from their selfishness."[48] How may we enter more into the perspective of others? A

[48] Gustavo Gutiérrez, *A Theology of Liberation* (Maryknoll, N.Y.: Orbis, 1973) 275.

variety of actions and of reflections can be helpful. I suggest that one helpful reflection is concerned with deepening an appreciation of our common experience of God, a liberating God who does not coerce and who does persuade.

In my philosophy I make explicit a third main characteristic of divine reverence: God does not use destructive coercion, only reverent persuasion. I reflect on four aspects. The idolatry of coercion should be rejected and the divine persuasion affirmed. God's fidelity to persuading and not coercing means divine openness to the experience of tragedy. Divine persuasion as a rule operates quietly. If there is need, God may wrestle with us; even then, divine persuasion uses no destructive or manipulative force.

In rejecting coercive idols and affirming divine persuasion, I use some of Whitehead's historical musement. The history could be qualified, but it still sheds light on typical fabrications about God. We attack three idols: "God in the image of an imperial ruler, God in the image of a personification of moral energy, God in the image of an ultimate philosophical principle."[49] The latter two images are idolatrous only in exaggerated or exclusive forms. A reverent God does not manipulate but is a source of moral energy who enlivens and invites us by divine beauty. A reverent God is not the only free actuality but is the ultimate philosophical principle in the sense of being the "only . . . non-derivative actuality."[50] The imperial ruler is the most problematic idol. "When the Western world accepted Christianity, Caesar conquered; and the received text of Western theology was edited by his lawyers."[51] This is hardly full or accurate history, yet it reminds us of the temptation to use coercion which Church leaders have recurrently faced and not always resisted. I agree with Whitehead that Christ's "brief Galilean vision of humility" centers on deeper truths. Christ's vision "dwells upon the tender elements in the world, which slowly and in quietness operate by love; and it finds purpose in the present immediacy of a kingdom not of this world."[52] In this text divine presence and cherishing are united with divine persuasion.

Within the development of Western religious thought which took place before Caesar conquered, Whitehead points to three peaks. The first is "Plato's publication of his final conviction . . . that the divine element in the world is to be conceived as a persuasive agency and not as a coercive agency."[53] The central moment is Christ's "revelation in act, of that

---

[49] PR 520.
[50] PR 48.
[51] PR 519.

[52] PR 520.
[53] AI 213.

which Plato divined in theory."[54] Thirdly, there is the theology of the Trinity, the Incarnation, and the Holy Spirit in which the Church Fathers suggested a metaphysical interpretation of how the divine persuasion might operate in the world.[55]

In my philosophy as in Whitehead's, God's fidelity to persuading and not coercing implies the divine acceptance of suffering from our evil choices and their results. "God is the great companion, the fellow-sufferer who understands."[56] As sufferer, God receives in intentional consciousness "each actual evil." As one who understands, God knows how evil may be overcome; by communicating that wisdom to us, God invites us to overcome evil so "as to issue in the restoration of goodness."[57] In so doing, God labors for the restoration of all goodness, including that of liberty, and not for the destruction of any goodness. "God's role is not the combat . . . of destructive force with destructive force; it lies in the patient operation of the overpowering rationality of his conceptual harmonization."[58] When God reverently challenges, we experience liberation. We are freed from the darkness of evil through the inspiration of God's "overpowering rationality," which can see a way out. We are liberated from the paralysis of evil through God's "tender patience leading . . . by his vision of truth, beauty, and goodness."[59] Because we experience God's leading, we can experience peace even in the midst of tragedy. This is a deep peace, not a psychic numbing which imagines that there exists no evil such as economic oppression or political torture. Rather, this peace is "a trust in the efficacy of Beauty,"[60] a confidence that God can lead us beyond evil to the restoration of goodness. This peace's "first effect is the removal of the stress of acquisitive feeling arising from the soul's preoccupation with itself,"[61] thus removal of a chief cause of injustice. "One of its fruits is that passion whose existence Hume denied, the love of mankind as such." [62] If we experienced God as coercive, then we would be defensive—preoccupied with self. Since God is persuasive, then on the deepest level we can live without being threatened, in holistic unity with God and with all humankind in one universal community.

How do we experience the divine persuasion? With Hocking I suggest that God persuades in two different ways appropriate to different directions of human movement. If we are basically growing from good to better, then God invites us with "a still, small voice."[63] When we progress, God speaks softly—partly to remind us of the divine reverence for our

---

[54] *AI* 214. See also Jon Sobrino, *Christology at the Crossroads* (Maryknoll: Orbis, 1978).
[55] *AI* 216. See also Sobrino.
[56] *PR* 532.
[57] *RM* 155.
[58] *PR* 525–26.
[59] *PR* 526.
[60] *AI* 367.
[61] *AI* 367.
[62] *AI* 368.
[63] *MG* 224.

freedom and invite us to reverence one another's freedom, partly to remind us that "Supreme Power" is "non-competitive ... —as Lao Tze glorifies the Tao that never asserts itself, as Christianity presents for adoration its God in the guise of an infant, an infant of the humblest."[64] God deals with us noncompetitively; we should deal with one another in like manner, even on a global level.

What if we are going from bad to worse? Then God does challenge us as a wrestler would—for our own strengthening. In such periods prayer means "that we maintain our discontent, returning again and again to the demand that our existence shall find itself justified in our own eyes.... This is the prayer of Jacob."[65] When we need to be awakened, God acts as an alarm clock. When we run away, the Hound of Heaven pursues. When we resist, God wrestles. God does not box, far less take up a sword or gun or bomb; that would be "destructive force." Rather God wrestles, strives, and suffers with us against evil, desiring not to harm us but to build us up for our overcoming evil. "Discontent" is experienced when "because of the God-nature within" those persons who need conversion *call themselves sinners* without losing self-respect or hope. Thanks to God's reverent wrestling, they experience the "tormenting joy" of "dwelling on sin," but "not in despair!"[66] God's reverent persuasion is not wishy-washy; God is faithful to the ideals which form part of the divine life, including the ideal of human freedom. Hence God reverently uses not destructive force but truth force, not coercion but persuasion.

At this period in history we citizens of the United States may hear the divine persuasion expressed through Latin American thinkers who challenge us to "dwell on sin" without losing hope. We may not be accustomed to theologians who write much about sinful facts and seemingly not much about ideal values; thus we may falsely imagine that they idealize class conflict. What they do is give an account of a class conflict already happening as a regrettable fact, then invite us to work together with them toward an ideal of reconciliation. "The Christian message demands that we move out of the whole schema of violence versus resistance to violence by the use of force as quickly as possible."[67] Violence includes starvation, torture, and threats. Violence is a sin, and "Resistance to violence is too, if it is adopted as a definitive attitude or if we allow ourselves to be taken over by its powerful dynamic. Christian redemption ... must derive its life from love."[68] Love seeks reconciliation and the

---

[64] *MG* 224.

[65] *MG* 436.

[66] *CWC* 106.

[67] Ignacio Ellacuria, *Freedom Made Flesh* (Maryknoll: Orbis, 1976) 229.

[68] Ibid. 229–30.

liberation of the oppressors as well as of the oppressed. "One loves the oppressors by liberating them from their inhuman condition as oppressors."[69] As a people some of whom export arms and a national-security mentality, we in the United States should be grateful that liberation theologians love us and seek to free us from an inhuman condition. Their wrestling is one medium of communication through which God's reverent persuasion reaches us. Our common human experience of that divine persuasion is the ground of the hope we all share.

CONCLUSION

Situating this work on divine reverence in the context of an inculturated North American philosophical theology, I chose to develop my ideas partly in dialogue with Hocking and Whitehead, the two philosophers who have influenced me most strongly. The two are central to the United States tradition of philosophizing about religious experience and of philosophizing which is relevant to reverence. Further historical articles or book chapters could develop other contributions from the tradition. I suggest some samples: Edwards and divine reverence in calling us through beauty, Transcendentalist reverence for holistic nature alternating with reverence for self-reliant individuals, reverent interpretive musement in Peirce and Royce, God's reverent invitation to conversion and saintliness in James, reverence in Royce's Suffering-Servant and Spirit-Interpreter, reverence for the community in Royce, creative and receptive reverence in Charles Hartshorne's dipolar philosophy of God, John Cobb and the God who reverently calls, reverence and liberation in Schubert Ogden's *Faith and Freedom*. I sincerely invite other members of the philosophical and theological community to join me in addressing the topic of divine reverence.

What might be most worth remembering from the present chapter? From its method, some equipment: (1) Musement—a key to release from the prison of merely formal understanding and reasoning, the freedom to let our feelings and imaginations play in God's beautiful out-of-doors. (2) Whole-aspect alternation—a camera with both a wide-angle lens for vista-vision and a zoom lens for detail. (3) Mystic-prophet alternation— a rhythm to keep ourselves fully alive, a way for prayer to nourish action and action to nourish prayer. From the chapter's main sections, some experiences: (1) God's reverent presence—sustaining,zest-giving,directing. (2) God's reverent cherishing—mirroring back our greatness, suffering at our side, and giving us hope that the way of the cross is part of the road to the resurrection. (3) God's reverent persuading—liberating us from coercive idols, speaking with the still and small voice when we

---

[69] Gutiérrez, *A Theology of Liberation* 276.

accept the invitation to grow, wrestling with us when we need the strength to accept a challenge to conversion.

What we have mystically contemplated about God's reverence for us invites us to show an analogous reverence for one another. Our prophetic deed of challenging the arms-makers, threateners, and torturers while supporting the food-makers, peacemakers, and justice-makers may have the lasting result of bringing our world-wide human community to fuller life, deeper reconcilation, and greater freedom. Yes, it involves risk. So does God's being present, cherishing, and persuading.

FRANK M. OPPENHEIM

Graced Communities:
A Problem in Loving

FRANK M. OPPENHEIM, S.J., is professor of philosophy at Xavier University in Cincinnati. He has specialized in the work of Josiah Royce and American philosophy, and is highly interested in ethics, especially business ethics. He is the author of *Royce's Voyage Down Under: A Journey of the Mind*, and of the forthcoming *Royce's Mature Philosophy of Religion*.

RELIGIOUS EXPERIENCE is at the heart of Josiah Royce's philosophy. His early "religious insight" of 1883 was a conviction about the reality of the All-Knower. It persisted throughout his life. In his final fifteen years (1902–16) he entered more and more into the "philosophy of life" movement. This led him to focus even more on divine life. In 1912, after his breakthrough to a maximal insight into C. S. Peirce's method and theory of signs, Royce expressed his mature thought most notably in his *The Problem of Christianity* (1913).[1] From then until his death he found the ideas of Spirit and community becoming increasingly life-giving and much more significant.[2] They enabled him to practice his new method—which I call "interpretive musement"—better than ever before.[3] It consisted in a free, playful, yet communally disciplined process

---

[1] J. Royce, *The Problem of Christianity* (2 vols.; New York: Macmillan, 1913); hereafter *Problem* in text, *PC* in notes; also available in reprints, esp. the one-volume edition (Chicago: University of Chicago, 1968). Except for Scripture citations, references within parentheses in the present article are to the 1913 edition: e.g., (1:xi–xii) = *PC*, Vol. 1, pp. xi–xii.— Already in 1918 Gabriel Marcel detected that *only* in Royce's later interpretative method of philosophizing had he finally (after having used less than effective instruments for so many years) succeeded in finding the *fitting medium* not only for communicating his message well but even for having it "essentially understood"; see Marcel, *Royce's Metaphysics* (Chicago: Regnery, 1956) 147.

[2] See Royce to Prof. Mary Whiton Calkins, March 20, 1916, *The Letters of Josiah Royce*, ed. John Clendenning (Chicago: University of Chicago, 1970) 644–648, esp. 645; hereafter *Letters*. In general, the mature Royce's idea of Spirit is as profound, pervasive, and analogical as is his idea of community. In 1915 Royce stated that his *sense* of "spirit" was not only "indeed Pauline" but also "perfectly capable of exact and logical statement" and thus Peircean; see J. Royce, *The Hope of the Great Community* (New York: Macmillan, 1916) 131; hereafter *HGC*. As Pauline, Royce's idea of Spirit was biblical and carried its "mystical, superindividual, and romantic" senses along with many others. It was "difficult to understand"; especially so, perhaps, if one tried to reduce to a fixed concept the "perfectly real, concrete, and literal life of what we idealists call the 'spirit' " (ibid.). As Peircean, this idea expressed itself in the logic of "communities of interpretation and of their spirit." Royce indicated to Prof. Warner Fite that the epsilon relation (whereby an individual entity *belongs* to a set) is the logical foundation for his theory of community. Lying behind this indication is the whole of Royce's distinctive logical System Sigma; see *Letters* 604–9, esp. 609, and *Royce's Logical Essays*, ed. D. S. Robinson (Dubuque: Wm. C. Brown, 1951) 350, 357, 377–78; hereafter *RLE*.

[3] For a description of interpretive musement, see further on in the text. For Royce's description of interpretation, as a third and irreducible mode of human knowing, see *PC* 2:109–221, esp. 158–63. Unlike perception and conception, interpretive knowing has for its object "minds and signs of minds." For example, a person tries to read his friend's unspoken

of knowing. Appreciatively sensitive to the living and ever fluent contexts of the communities about him, he sought to win close personal touch with "minds and signs of minds," whether these took him into the realms of ethics or logic, scientific methodology or international insurance.

Most Americans scarcely recognize the name Josiah Royce. Among those who do, most have discarded him with stereotypes that quickly foreclose genuine listening to him, especially in his mature period (1912–16). He has been labeled "idealist" (in any of a half-dozen senses), "Hegelian" (although he disallowed this: e.g., in 1:xi–xii), "absolutist," "pneumatologist" (because of his mature emphasis on the Spirit),[4] "too Germanic" (although he was the son of '49ers and prided himself on being a Californian), "overintellectualistic," and so forth.

Where do these denigrating remarks come from? Given the way the mature Royce grew more ready to admit his limits (2:336), these remarks seem to me not to derive from a careful and critically balanced study of the "new light . . . new experience" that Royce saw had produced his "essentially new aspect of philosophical idealism" (2:422).[5] Rather, they have far oftener proven to be beams in the beholder's eye than real specks in Royce's.

---

preference, or a translator tries to grasp from the Hebrew text the genuine intent of Isaiah and convey it faithfully to an English reader, or a banker tries to discern through the varied signs connected with a candidate for a loan the latter's reliability. Consisting in a cognitive process rather than a single act, interpretation is distinctive because, operating in a field of signs, its basic logical structure is not dyadic (subject-object), as in perception and conception, but triadic (threefold): from sign-sender through sign-interpreter to sign-receiver.

[4] See n. 2 above and n. 9 below. Although some theologians accept the Pauline-Johannine notion of *pneuma* without qualm, they may feel uneasy with the mature Royce's admittedly Pauline-Johannine idea of Spirit (*PC* 2:16; *Letters* 646). Various factors, working singly or together, may produce this uneasiness. (1) Since many have cut their first theological teeth on the bones of modern (rather than contemporary) European philosophical thought, a theologian so trained may tend to stay within his or her almost purely intellectualistic context rather than leap into that aesthetico-pragmatic-cognitive ambience of American philosophy, which understanding Royce calls for. (2) Although knowing that such American philosophers of religion as James, Royce, and Hocking belong to the "philosophy of life" movement, a person may neither center empathetically on *life* nor deal with Royce's idea of life at that "higher than third level of Peircean clarification" which suits it. (3) Instead of adopting the mature Royce's interpretational (triadic) mode of knowing, one may fixate in a subject-object (dyadic) epistemology. (4) Although knowing that, for the late Royce, a "fundamental idea" is a highly dynamic "sign of mind guiding an interpretive process," one may try to reduce Royce's idea of spirit to a mere concept. (5) The life of the divine Spirit, whether in human minds and human communities or in Itself, not only eludes ultimate definition but is a disquieting mystery. Any of these factors, then, will prevent a broad, coherent, yet intimate insight into Royce's "indeed Pauline" sense of "spirit" and seed the uneasiness of misunderstanding this idea.

[5] *Letters* 645.

If one expects that the mature Royce's professedly Christian philosophy of religion had to draw upon the New Testament, he might reasonably inquire how competent and accurate was Royce in hermeneutics and New Testament exegesis. This question would have surprised Royce; for in his final years he saw himself mainly as a comparative methodologist, a logician, and a Christian ethician and metaphysician rather than as a Scripture scholar (1:x, xxix; 2:15–16). However, some recent investigators highly appraise Royce's achievement and accuracy even in hermeneutics and exegesis. For example, German scholar Karl-Otto Apel sees Royce's mature work in the theory of hermeneutics as indispensable: "Royce's idea of the 'community of interpreters,' expounded in the second volume of his last [major] work, *The Problem of Christianity* (1913), provides perhaps the most important single contribution to the extension and development in hermeneutic and social philosophical terms of Peirce's semiotic."[6] Concerning Royce's competence as an interpreter of the New Testament, Dieter Georgi, Frothingham Professor of Biblical Studies at Harvard Divinity School, sums up his appraisal as follows: "In the *Problem*, then, Royce sensed and stressed the corporate and historical dynamisms at work within the interpretation process more concretely and skillfully than Bultmann or Heidegger have done. For these reasons, in his mature work, Royce considerably surpassed Bultmann as an interpreter of the New Testament."[7]

Reassured by such recommendations, we can investigate Royce's question whether we should love graced communities as such. Our main investigation seeks a Roycean exegesis of the apostle Paul's descriptions of how his early Christian communities were led to transform Jesus' doctrine of love. It then presents three philosophical reasonings on this question. It concludes by highlighting three points: the shift in method employed, a fitting way of translating Royce's answer into practice, and an application of his answer to the justice area. However, before this main investigation, we first need to familiarize ourselves with a central theme and some basic terms in the mature Royce. Thus equipped, we can fittingly enter Royce's method of interpretation and then through it detect the Pauline development of the early Christian doctrine of love.

In the *Problem* Royce identified the highest human good with one's transformation under grace into an essentially new life (1:171, 207, 345,

[6] Karl-Otto Apel, *Charles S. Peirce: From Pragmatism to Pragmaticism* (Amherst: University of Massachusetts, 1981) 135. Robert S. Corrington finds Royce offering "a more general analysis of interpretation than anyone before him"; see his "Royce's Community of Interpretation: The Horizon of Hermeneutics" (unpublished dissertation, Drew University, Madison, N.J., 1982) ii.

[7] Georgi's 1982 Foreword (vii) to Oppenheim, *Royce's Mature Philosophy of Religion* (University of Notre Dame Press), announced for Fall, 1986.

405). The individualistic self is deeply alienated and morally detached from any genuine community. For example, when a passionate careerist encounters the pressures and institutions of society, he becomes more tense and hostile, even as he becomes more sophisticated in winning his ends, despite others. Further contacts, either with manipulators more powerful than himself (e.g., organized crime) or with the disabled or uncouth or outcasts of society, only make him more dedicated to his own career, without time or care for others. But one day he chances on a loyal community (perhaps a truly loving family open to the needs of others). Under its influence he comes to the point of committing himself whole-heartedly to the shared life of this community with its universal openness. This conversion to genuine loyalty also leads him to promote the birth or growth of genuine loyalty in all other minded beings he can touch. Just as grace was needed for his moral transformation, so his new life of practically serving the overall interest of his new community needs grace to maintain and foster it. He could wilfully violate the living unity with his fellow loyalists by not following the superhuman source of that unity (i.e., by "sinning against the Holy Spirit"). His genuine loyalty reaches full maturity the day he enters into his community's atonement process to heal wounded community life and restore lost individualists to the unity of genuinely loyal life. In sum, Royce understands conversion as a process of interpretation occurring between an individualist, a saving community, and its Spirit (1:xvi; 2:312–13).

The taproot of Royce's mature thought is his distinction between two essentially different levels both of reality and of consciousness: the level of the individual and that of the genuine community (1:343, 405).[8] An individual is the unique object of a knowing and affirmative interest which constitutes a self as "be-loved"—ultimately be-loved by the divine Spirit. If the individual is united through transforming loyalty to a level of existence that is essentially higher than his own grade of individualist being, he is on the way to his highest good—as we just observed with the converted careerist. Otherwise he is a lost individual, at least for the time being (1:405).

A community is different from a society or a social institution. A human community requires not only considerable temporal process but also appreciatively shared memories of idealized past events, along with communally shared hopes of anticipated and enhanced life together (2:57–69, 99–103). In a society, by contrast, this shared awareness of common idealized past and future events may or may not be present.

---

[8] Pointing out the relation between the traditional doctrine of Christ's "two natures" and his own thesis about the "two levels," Royce claimed sole responsibility for asserting this relation; see PC 1:203, n. 1.

And in a social institution, taken simply as a group's consensually established way of procedure, these shared awarenesses will not be present; for a society's only requisites are the mutual acceptance of some purpose and the co-operative organization of means to achieve it, and the requisite for a social institution is simply a consensus that establishes a procedure.

Human communities arise spontaneously but are caught in historical antecedents and societal pressures. Thus they tend defensively to prefer their own interests. So communities, such as a family or clan or nation, tend to build up loyalties that are naturally exclusivistic. As natural, these closed or chauvinistic communities lack a moral commitment to all human selves and to all genuine communities. Natural communities need to be transformed at least as much as their morally detached individualistic members.

By contrast, genuinely loyal communities seek a universal cause and promote the rise of genuine loyalty in all minded beings. But such communities can begin and be maintained only by grace "as from above" (2:102). There exists, then, both a highest Beloved Community and its Spirit-Interpreter. From them derive all humanly embodied finite beloved communities (e.g., graced family, genuine Church).

A human family, then, may be either a merely natural community or a genuine community, depending on whether its members are only naturally (= exclusivistically) dedicated to the family or are universally loyal. Communities are seriated by grades into small, intermediate, great, and universal. The "Great Community" embraces all human beings of all time. The "Universal Community" embraces all minded beings of all time (e.g., God, angels, humans, and possibly other minds). When viewed as graced, the universal community is called the "Beloved Community" in its greatest scope, whereas a Pauline church and the worldwide Christian Community (insofar as graced) would be instances of small or intermediate beloved communities respectively.

Aware of the moral disorder at work in merely natural human communities, we can appreciate Royce's care to clarify exactly what he meant and did not mean by his second or saving level of reality—which he called "man the spiritual community" (2:406). To forestall misidentifications of this key term, Royce first eliminated counterfeit candidates: not the collective biological population called the human race; not ourselves as a culturally trained community whose members, as socialized animals, are guided simply by customs and conventional do's and don't's; not humanity viewed as a series of historical adventures, some tragic, some successful. Rather, Royce specified, by man the spirtual community "I mean man in the sense in which Paul conceived Christ's beloved and universal Church to be a community,—man viewed as one conscious spiritual whole of life ... the essential source of the salvation of the individual" (1:405–6). This community, intended for all human selves, is beloved by the Spirit of Christ,[9] constitutes "the realm of grace," and already embodies seminally the announced kingdom of heaven to come.

After this introduction to Royce and to some of his basic ideas, we seem prepared to consider an issue central to his religious philosophy: whether we should love graced communities as such. In gist, Royce's argument is that the highest human good consists in every human individual's being transformed from his attitude of isolated and immoral self-preference into becoming a loyal member of a universal community. Each does this by committing himself wholeheartedly to deeds of service to some beloved nonexclusivistic community. For this transformation and growing practical service to occur, two conditions must be met. The human individual must be empowered to love the beloved community as

---

[9] See nn. 2 and 4 above. Royce identified Christ with the "spirit of the Church" and with the "spirit of the universal community" (PC 1:206, 212, 354; 2:16), and identified the name "Christ" with the symbol of the Spirit that unifies Christians (PC 2:425–28). These Roycean usages derive from the "Christ = Spirit" formulas of the early Pauline letters and reflect an early theology of many Christians in the apostolic churches (PC 1:187, 192, 196). Without reading dogmatic statements about the Trinity into PC, one can fittingly interpret Royce's identification of Christ with the spirit of the Church (and with the spirit of the universal community) in terms of a dynamic and/or teleological identity.—In systematic Trinitarian theology a binatarian is one who identifies the glorified Christ in personal supposit (in hypostasi) with the other Paraclete and then, mutually opposing this one Person to the Father, holds only two Persons in the one divine nature. To raise the question whether Royce is a binatarian is to mistake him for a systematic theologian, to exceed textual evidence, and to violate his nonontological style of thought.—Although Royce's imprecision on just which kind of identity he attributes to Christ and the "spirit of the universal community" may be a neuralgic point for some dogmatic theologians, it keeps windows open for other thinkers; for it can remind them of the often unnoticed imprecision of their own usages of "spirit" and invite them to explore more carefully into Royce's many senses of "spirit." Concerning our senses of "Spirit," even when limited in its application only to the God of the Christians, we say "Spirit" of God when the divine reality is viewed either as one or as triune. We can designate the Father or Son or Holy Spirit as "Spirit." And even when referring to the Trinity's economy of saving the human race through the Word and the Third Person, we can say "Spirit" of either "Sent One" whether viewed in an eternal ad intra reality or in a historic mission in world process. Nor have we as yet even surveyed our usages of "spirit" for created realities, where imprecision may abound yet more.—Concerning Royce's refined senses of "spirit," his most frequent usage of the term designates finite individuals and their communities: e.g., "the human spirit" or "the spirit of [humankind's] Great Community." (See my article "The Idea of Spirit in the Mature Royce," Transactions of the C. S. Peirce Society 19, no. 4 [Fall 1983]). More rarely, Royce used "Spirit" to symbolize the divine nature itself (PC 2:15–16, 219–20). Hence to be uneasy that more havoc may come from Royce's usages of "Spirit" than from our own seems both to show less confidence in the "Spirit of the Church" than Royce had and to forget his directive that genuinely loyal persons need to "discern spiritually the things of the spirit" (PC 2:361).

a reality distinct from, and higher than, any human individual. He must also, through his genuine loyalty towards the universal community, come to love its every human member, actual and potential.

HOW DID PAUL TRANSFORM JESUS' DOCTRINE OF LOVE?

The better to enter into Royce's interpretation of the early development of the Christian doctrine of love, we will follow his own three major steps. (1) We will describe the external and internal contexts for this development. That is, just what was the *preaching* of Jesus which impinged upon the early Christian communities of interpretation? And in Jesus' early followers, what was the internal set of simple human *motives* (psychological, aesthetical, and ethical) which moved these first Christians to love communities as such? (2) With Royce we will expose Jesus' doctrine of love. (3) We will trace how, in mutual interaction with the early Christian communities, Paul transformed Jesus' doctrine to include love for the Church as such, as well as love for individuals.[10]

External and Internal Contexts (1:49–74)

The doctrine of Christian love originates from Jesus' love for his Father and for his Father's kingdom of heaven—that "union of the blessed with their Father" (1:50). From Jesus' two-leveled love sprang his central teaching about the Father and about that fundamental social entity which he and his Father love. This doctrine is the life-giving seed contained in Jesus' various parables.

During the apostolic age, then, the followers of Jesus had to interpret just what this kingdom meant for them. Experiencing the Spirit of the risen Lord active in their assemblies, they were led to the shared awareness that Jesus meant the kingdom of heaven to be made real among themselves by their co-operative choices. This was to occur *in* the felt union (koinonia) of the faithful, *through* the guidance of his Spirit leading them, and *for* their future experience whenever the Master returned (1:50). In brief, the explicit birthing of the idea of the Church and of its mission arose from the earliest Christians' desire to follow Jesus' teaching about the kingdom. Their desire led them in practice to embody this teaching by deeds of consciously co-operative life. They believed that this communal life of theirs was being guided into the future by the Spirit towards a judgment by the Master on his return.

Expanding our focus to include human selves of any time and place— whether or not they have heard the Christian doctrine of love—we begin with Royce to reflect carefully and critically on the interacting sets of

---

[10] Here I rely mainly on *PC*'s second lecture "The Idea of the Universal Community" (1:49–106), drawing assistance from its fourth and tenth lectures ("The Realm of Grace" and "The Body and the Members").

motives which lead any human beings to become conscious of both the idea and the ideal of a universal community (which includes all minded beings: human, angelic, divine, etc.). We can discover how this consciousness arises by alternating our focus between the psychological and the ethico-aesthetic motives which lead towards this idea and ideal. Hence, to identify the psychological motives first, we start with ordinary people's encounters with small-size communities and then with larger ones (1:61–63).

For example, people notice how a ship's crew co-operate to set sail or how the members of a well-trained orchestra work together. Upon experiencing groups like these which act for a purpose, people are moved psychologically to adopt three beliefs. (1) These social groups somehow have a *life* of their own, different from the lives of individual members. (2) Somehow, too, each of these groups has a *mind* of its own, evident from its correction of straying members. (3) These social groups *tend to* form communities of *higher levels* (e.g., linking family to clan to tribe, or uniting churches at local, regional, and universal levels). If members encounter strangers unfamiliar with the members' language, rites, crafts, or other customs, they become conscious that their own tribal (or other) community has indeed a life of its own and a mind of its own. Its social products (language, rites, customs, etc.) show this communal life and mind as convincingly as an individual's handshake reveals his own individual life and mind.

But as soon as one recognizes these psychological motives which lead people to think of their social groups as distinct from individuals, objectors immediately protest: "Don't personify or 'thingify' or idealize communities!" "Remember they are *merely* operational unities." Responding like Royce, we confine ourselves at this stage to a simple working hypothesis. Without yet expressing any metaphysical theory, we will proceed by treating these living purposeful communities as if they had their own life and mind.

Focusing next on ethico-aesthetic motives in people everywhere, we find that all of them do more than form the above-mentioned three beliefs about the social groups they live in (1:66–74). They also love their families, serve their religious groups, live and even die for their nation. They appreciate these communities as somehow having more value than their individual lives alone. In their family and "church" and nation they find something that calls them to right rather than wrong choice. Also in these groups they can and often do find something beautiful, even sublime. And they show that they detect when their common life is healthy and growing, as well as when it becomes sick or even degenerate.

These ethico-aesthetic motives, as well as the psychological ones, are irrepressible in the human psyche's operations. These motives lead both to the idea of a level of life higher than that of any separated individual and also to the ideal of a universal community—first, of all human persons, and later, of all minded persons. This ideal arises from the tendency to form higher levels of community and to find something increasingly powerful, beautiful, and sublime in them. Thus the idea and ideal of the universal community is just as irrepressible in the human psyche as is its desire for the true, the good, and the beautiful.

Royce had set the contexts—the one which surrounded Jesus' teaching in the early Christian assemblies of the apostolic age, the other which underlies the psyche of every potential hearer of that doctrine. Because the human psyche is irrepressibly motivated to produce and treasure the idea and ideal of the universal community, it is a well-attuned human matrix for the doctrine of the kingdom. Royce was ready, then, to show how Jesus' doctrine of love depends on the doctrine of the kingdom.

Jesus' Doctrine of Love (1:74–91)

As contained in Jesus' sayings and parables, his doctrine of Christian love is based on the Father's love for each individual human person. The Father regards and loves each person as a member of the kingdom of heaven and as one destined to its fulness (1:197–98). Since the Father makes His sun shine and rain fall on good and evil people alike, Jesus develops the Old Testament doctrine of love by expanding its scope to include even one's "enemies." As Royce portrays Jesus' doctrine, "One is to love one's neighbor because God himself, as Father, divinely loves and prizes each individual man. Hence the individual man has an essentially infinite value, although he has this value only in and through his relation to God, and because of God's love for him" (1:80).

Just as the Jesus of the sayings rejoices in the Father's love for each person, so he invites everyone to rejoice in the consciousness of this love itself and to delight in all people, since they too are God's beloveds. Because love is divine in its origin and goal, it includes an assertion of each person's relatedness to God, "for the God who loves me demands . . . that I should be his own" (1:81). Strengthened by the Father's great love for him and eagerly anticipating the final victory of God's will, one recognizes that his first duty is to promote love in all, to extend the kingdom by teaching love to all (1:85). To do this when encountering the evils of life, he also needs to extend emphathetic mercy to those in misery, as the Father does. In brief, Jesus' doctrine of love is positive, strenuous, even heroic. It makes simplified popularizations of it—like "Have no thought for oneself " or "Live wholly for others"—shrivel up in their own inadequacy before the genuine sunshine of this doctrine.

In it, however, Jesus left something unclarified, even while wanting his Spirit-led people to discover and develop a right way to engage in practical activity in society. He wanted that way to be both genuinely loving and yet well ordered. For example, if an early Christian simplistically interpreted the golden rule to mean that he was to satisfy his neighbor's needs, what would result? He would soon discover that it is not his own call to meet all those needs. But how discern which needs he should meet, which not? Here the early Christian communities found a task for interpretation and communicated their findings to Paul.

Paul's Transformation of This Doctrine (1:91–106)

"Paul" in Royce means the Paul of Romans, of 1 and 2 Corinthians, of Galatians, Philippians, and 1 Thessalonians.[11] According to Royce, the experiences that Paul had with the early Christian communities taught him first to conceive of "church" in reference to the local Christian assembly (e.g., at Damascus, Antioch, Jerusalem, Philippi, etc.). Only gradually did he become aware of the body of Christ as a universal corporate reality (1:104).

Paul found each local church small enough that it kept all its members in touch with one another, particularly through their worship assemblies. Accepting and trusting one another, they became aware through their communications not only of the physical needs, dangers, works, and successes of each member, but also of the way these were related to the health of the whole body of Christ locally present (1:102). In this way Paul gradually came to experience the local church as a perceptible institutional instrument for fulfilling his Master's intent about the kingdom. He found this intent being embodied in many of his missionary locales. Everywhere he went it fitted in neatly with people's deepest interests. He gradually became aware that this intent was to be realized in a world-wide body.

Paul faithfully transmitted Jesus' doctrine on love. In 1 Corinthians 13 he expressed this doctrine more completely than anywhere else in the

---

[11] Royce's acquaintance with the Scripture scholarship of his decades schooled him to distinguish ordinarily between Paul's authentic writings and the NT writings that stem from Christians in the "Pauline tradition." Moreover, by concentrating on Christianity's earliest writings, Royce transmitted the Pauline Paul (of the authentic letters) and did not encapsulate him in the Lucan Paul of the Acts (which Royce did not use for Pauline exegesis). Yet he also relied upon the fourth Gospel and Ephesians (esp. Eph 5:25–28) for his interpretation of Jesus and early Christianity. Present-day refinements of seventy further years of scriptural scholarship may thus find some remnants of fundamentalism in Royce. But he had his reasons for relying as heavily upon Ephesians and the fourth Gospel as he did upon Paul's earliest letters. His reasons were Christian tradition and integrity of view; for he recognized that traditionally Christians have imbibed their Jesus more from the fourth Gospel than from the Synoptics. Moreover, he realized that Ephesians and the fourth Gospel present Jesus and his mission with more of an insightful meditative wholeness than do the Synoptics. See PC 1:206.

New Testament. Yet Paul's letters also reveal an inevitable development of this doctrine; for in them the term "neighbor" often becomes "fellow member" of the Christian community. These letters show Christ loving his bride, the Church, as well as individual Christians. Jesus had sacrificed himself for her, willing gradually to transform her into a fully beautiful reality (Eph 5:25–28). Similarly, those faithful to Christ are called to love this new corporate reality which he has united to himself in the Spirit. Thus, besides God and the individual human persons, Paul explicitly proposed another kind of being to be loved: the Church as Christ's bride. The whole value of each Christian as an individual hangs on his membership in this body of Christ; for outside it he is lost (1:97). Let each live together, then, in such a way that their assembly both be worthy of the Christ who loves it and simultaneously "so help the individual brother that he may be a fitting member of the Church" (1:103).

Because Christ dedicated himself wholeheartedly for his Church as well as for each member in it, his love is that of "graced loyalty." Accordingly, each Christian's love should be formed by "graced loyalty." Jesus imitated his Father's love for both the whole human community summoned to salvation and for every unique human person called to salvation in and through that community. So by his espousal covenant with his bride, Jesus, the servant of the Father and of humankind, became one new reality with her, an instrument for the salvation of all. Hence the individual Christian's love should include, besides commitment to God, neighbor, and self, a graced loyalty towards the Father's Beloved Community as embodied in the spousal covenant between Christ and transformable humankind. That is, the individual Christian's affective and practical dedication to the Church should be so wholeheartedly loving as to be atoning (or paschal). The maturation of a genuine Christian's graced loyalty toward the Church inevitably evokes the courageous will to follow Christ faithfully and resolutely into deeds of Father-like charity and of atonement and through them into a fuller life for all (1:xix-xx, 43–44, 322–23; 2:377).

Paul recognized that his Christians experienced, sometimes even perceptibly, the "unity of the Spirit" binding them into one body (1:74). Through reciprocal influence, this unity was both source and fruit of these Christians' genuine loyalty and atoning deeds in, with, and for the Church. In the Spirit which generated such unity Paul also recognized the glorified Lord who was both divine life and head of the Christian communities (1:104).[12] What Paul's quantum leap in explicitating the

[12] See n. 9 above.

doctrine of Christian love consisted in, then, can be grasped more clearly if we muse over Royce's own summary:

In God's love for the neighbor, the parables [of Jesus] find the proof of the infinite worth of the individual. In Christ's love for the Church Paul finds the proof that both the community and the individual member are the objects of an infinite concern, which glorifies them both, and thereby unites them. The member finds his salvation only in union with the Church. He, the member, would be dead without the divine spirit and without the community. But the Christ whose community this is, has given life to the members—the life of the Church, and of Christ himself. 'You hath he quickened, which were dead in trespasses and sins.'[13]

In sum: Christian love, as Paul conceives it, takes on the form of Loyalty. This is Paul's simple but vast transformation of Christian love. (1:98)

MUSEMENTS SUPPORTING LOVE FOR COMMUNITIES AS SUCH

For centuries many Christians have had a great deal of love for the Church and not merely a love for individual Christians in the Church. As just seen, Royce interpreted how Paul developed Jesus' doctrine of love into a doctrine that included a love for graced communities as such. Yet, as far as my sampling permits a tentative generalization, most theologians have not attended directly to the complementary and yet distinctive kind of love presupposed by Paul's development of Jesus' doctrine of Christian love.[14] Alerted by the contrast between Royce's

[13] Eph 2:1.

[14] Guided by Walter J. Burghardt, Avery Dulles, and Joseph A. Fitzmyer (to whom I owe thanks but not the onus of responsibility for this report), I sounded out some leading theologians on Royce's question: Should graced individuals, besides loving all individual persons, also love graced communities as such? This question is clarified if we first develop it positively. E.g., does the Charity Christ breathes into his members impel them not only to love God, self, and neighbor as individuals, but also to love graced communities as such? Or again, if Christ redemptively loves his bride the Church, should his Christians redemptively love all graced communities as minded beings that image his Father's Trinitarian Community of Life? This question is brought into still sharper focus if we put it negatively. E.g., if the objects of a person's love are *only* God, neighbor, and myself, viewed as individuals, but not graced communities, viewed as communions in the Spirit, is the healthy, well-ordered development of that person's love severely blocked or, at best, held in immaturity? In my pioneer research into theologians on this question, I sampled pertinent passages in systematicians (de Lubac, G. Gilleman, James Gustafson, Richard McBrien, Karl Rahner, and Eduard Schillebeeckx), in exegetes (Marcus Barth, Joseph Fitzmyer, Victor Furnish, and Juan Luis Segundo), and in students of pneumatology (Yves Congar, Hans Küng, Jürgen Moltmann, and Heribert Mühlen). Tentatively, I read the meaning of this sample as follows. Like the Fathers, these theologians often refer to the mystery of the Church, to faith in it, and to dedicated service to it. Taking the Trinity (formed by the Holy Spirit as the "We" of the Father and of the Son) for his paradigmatic Community, Mühlen applies this model by analogy first to Christ (the "We" of the Logos and of humankind-to-be-redeemed) and then to the Church (the "We" of Christ and of

exegesis and this apparent theological lacuna, we can bring the interpretive process of this essay to completion by comparing and contrasting the foregoing Roycean interpretation of Paul's doctrine of love with some reasonings built upon a philosophy of the Christian religion. Accordingly, after briefly describing the method of interpretative musement, I will, as a philosopher of the Christian religion, try to find and create a trio of musements upon the central question of the present study. I hope they will be a trio of consistent and cogent reasonings which, when united with Royce's exegesis of Paul, will illumine that question.

In general, Royce teaches that Christian love for those realities which are genuine human communities must focus directly upon them qua beloved communities. It must not love these communities only indirectly and derivatively, as if they were simply the sum of their individual members, loved as individuals. Of course, love for individual persons is always required; yet it is never enough for genuine Christian love. Christians' love of God as undivided Unity in Three Persons is paradigmatic; for when this love bears upon the Trinity, it should focus directly upon the divine life in community, the shared divine koinonia, rather than directly upon any one or all of the Three Persons, even though Christians' love of the Father and Son and Holy Spirit as Three Persons is clearly also essential to their love of God. According to Royce, then, Paul taught that Christians' love should take part in the love that Christ their head had, not only for each individual but also for the sacred communions in God, in the kingdom, in Christ, in the Church, and in humankind as redeemed.

The Method of Interpretative Musement

Theologians should profitably notice philosophers of religion, especially if the problems the latter raise and the approaches they take

---

humankind-as-graced-and-instrumentally-redemptive). Gilleman and de Lubac, by focusing on the Trinity's koinonia and on the Pauline *mystērion* respectively, closely approach, yet do not directly address themselves to, Royce's question. In his *Theological Investigations* Karl Rahner also approaches this question both in Vol. 5 and in his recently Englished Vol. 20, "Concern for the Church," yet does not treat it directly. In sum, I found no theologian dealing directly with Royce's question about the ethico-religious exigence to love graced communities as communal realities on a higher-than-individual level. Furthermore, I found no theologian asserting with Royce that the only way in which love for individuals can become rightly ordered is if that love is transformed by a love for graced communities as such and if it operates in the ambience of such a community's felt saving love for oneself. One's love for individuals, then, participates in the Three Persons' *kind* of love for Their uncreated Beloved Community and for all created individuals insofar as these are destined for the created kingdom of God which is being realized through world history by the well-ordered love and action of the Trinitarian Community working *ad extra* in a redemptive way.

promise to cast light on important theological questions. As a philosopher of religion, Royce raised a problem about the adequacy of traditional interpretations of Christian love; yet his problem has not been directly attended to by the theologians I surveyed.[15] In my turn, as a philosopher of religion, I am here inviting theologians to the adventure of breaking away from the captivating paths of professionalized mental routines and to an experiment in interpretive musement as an alternate way of theological reflection.

What happens when a theologian muses like Royce or Peirce upon a mystery, such as God, or Christ, or Church, or Holy Spirit? Procedurally, his will-to-interpret promotes a deepening familiarity with the mystery. His search for a fuller understanding of the mystery will be furthered by comparing and contrasting different perspectives on the mystery. He will enter these perspectives by alternating the fundamental categories which he uses to approach the mystery. This will lead, gradually and serially, to a discerning familiarity with the mystery, a familiarity that becomes increasingly adequate and interpersonally disciplined.

For instance, one can seek this kind of familiarity with the mystery of Christ's Church if one reverently and rhythmically employs such pairs of ideas as "human" *and* "divine," "temporal" *and* "eternal," "mind" *and* "sign of mind," "individual" *and* "community," "self-identical entity" *and* "ever-fluent process," etc. By comparing and contrasting the interpretations of the Church which thus arise, one can enter into a knowledge of it that is increasingly concrete and personally challenging.[16]

To engage in musement like this, one needs to insist from the start on making room for freely playing with possibilities. One needs to resist any a priori channeling of this adventure in musement on mystery. Thus from the start one needs to stand firm against initiating the raising of questions, against slipping into some oft-tried method, against settling down into a familiar mood supposedly conducive to doing theology, and against accepting traditional formulae without context or critical discernment. These taboos are needed if one is to avoid imposing control upon the mysterious life in which one muses by receiving signs. Positively, this adventure in musement calls one to be sensitively free and imaginatively creative. It calls one to play freely with possibilities with alert receptivity and inner novelty, both in solitude and with others. In this way one will begin comparing and contrasting successive pairs of "signs" and thus learn how to engage in a mental dance by rhythmically alter-

---

[15] See n. 14 above.

[16] The fathers of the Second Vatican Council engaged in a somewhat similar comparison-contrast of alternative perspectives in their Constitution on the Church, esp. at the close of no. 9. See *The Documents of Vatican II*, ed. Walter M. Abbott, S.J. (New York: America, 1966) 26.

nating one's steps. We hinted at this mental dancing in our example above of musement on the mystery of the Church.

Interpretive musement is valuable. By requiring love of genuine community for this musing on mystery, interpretive musement roots thinkers in *caritas*; for one must loyally love not only individual persons but also the created and Trinitarian communities in which the divine Spirit ministers as their Source of unity and love. Such musement also liberates thinkers from absolutizing one or other metaphysical position. It highlights how inadequate is any position that poses as a statement of the comprehensive truth about reality.

Musements That Support Love for Graced Communities as Such

As grist for his reasonings, a philosopher of religion can borrow Christian beliefs—say, about the Trinity or providence—without giving or expecting a faith-assent to them. The starting points for the three following musements, then, will be the Trinity's causality *ad extra*, the nature of the Third Person as the indwelling bond of the Triune Community, and the dynamisms deeply at work in an individual if examined as simply a human person or as also a beloved child of grace.

Our first musement will start from the Trinity's *ad extra* action of creating finite minded individuals. Our analogous knowledge of an agent focuses on three moments in his action.[17] With awareness of possibilities and free commitment, a minded agent is receptive to the attraction of something valuable (some good) and adopts it as his own intended goal. (We indicate this influence upon the agent by the goal intended and his correlative orientation of mind by the shorthand expression "final causality.") Then, as an aid needed for guiding the (at least partial) attainment of this goal, the minded agent creates or finds in his awareness some model or exemplar of the action or artifact which he intends to produce when carrying out his intent. (We indicate this moment of sign-creation by "exemplary causality.") Lastly, through choice and physical activity, the agent actually produces this action or artifact within some historical processing community. (We indicate this production, in a

---

[17] Here our Royce-like presupposition is a process of communicating life that occurs between real, individual, minded members of a community who address, interpret, and cooperate with one another. Set in this communitarian context, our resultant interpretation of causality as paradigmatically found in the many-phased process of vital interpersonal communication differs significantly from some traditional causal notions: e.g., from Aristotle, who made the individual organism his paradigmatic causal agent and thus inverted priorities, as well as from Hume and Kant, whose nominalistic phenomenism precluded "close personal touch" with the two kinds of real mutual interaction between members themselves and between a community and its members. See *RLE* 161, 193.

shorthand phrase, by "efficient causality" or "agent causality.") And so, to our first musement.

1) Suppose that the supreme reality is a Trinity of Persons in one nature, an uncreated intersubjective communion (koinonia) in which life, knowledge, and love are communicated. Suppose, too, that this divine community freely intends, is the exemplar of, and actually produces a universe of created minded beings. Suppose, finally, that antecedent to creation the only reality and value is this Trinitarian community in its goodness.

Then, according to final causality, the only goodness which this un-created koinonia can value and intend is its own living community. But then, if this Trinity of Persons actually intends to create finite minds, the latter have to be linked inextricably to the Trinity's own Beloved Community, Its sole goodness. Such linkage is possible for finite minds, however, only if these latter are intrinsically directed to some finite communion which circulates life, knowledge, and love, in a finite likeness of Trinitarian communion, in a created "kingdom of God."

Furthermore, according to exemplary causality, the creative art of the divine community will guide its *ad extra* creative agency, according to its finite sign or model of the divine community. Thus the Trinity's making and developing of any universe will accord with this internal meaning or guiding sign which will be unavoidably present and at work in any created reality, whether rational or subrational; for just as on the infinite level the Father cannot be Father unless He expresses His life in His Son who reflects Him infinitely, so the divine Community, if It chooses to express Its Reality on a finite level, can do so only as guided by a finite community-like "sign" or model which reflects the only Reality God is, that divine koinonia of an intersubjective communion wherein life, knowledge, and love are circulated. At its own level, then, the created universe should be a beloved community and one fittingly composed of an ascending series of finite beloved communities.

Finally, according to that kind of agent causality proper to Three Persons co-operating in Their action of creation, the life, knowledge, and love characteristic of the unity of these "Three Conspirators *ad extra*" must coconstitute the unique free choice which brings the finite universe into being and process. Their free conspiring in one Will-to-interpret Their Community in finite style integrates existential choice, playful wisdom, and infectious joy. This conspiracy holds in being and process a real, universal, but finite community that includes as one of its real levels the great human community with all its members. Fittingly, then, did Royce concur with Peirce in musing about our universe as a community in which "the nature of things" (life-giving fatherly firstness) is bonded to "attuned minded beings" (factual filial secondness) by a "third world of signs" (integrating spiritual thirdness); for the universal finite community of these three interlinked "worlds" provides for minds that stand in loyal love of the universe and that ponder the linkages of these "worlds" a sufficient clue of that triadic community of agency from whose life, mind, and unitive love our universe arises (2:395, 411).

We find this musement confirmed if we next contrast the three foregoing reasonings against our existing world. Despite disorders and community breakdowns, we find that communal life among finite minded beings emerges abundantly. There are families, linguistic-economic-cultural communities, the Church, and the presently hoped-for "great community" of all humankind. Consequently, if one desires the coming of God's kingdom even in its temporal anticipations but fails to love and serve these created communities as bodies divinely intended to aid humankind's temporal advance towards the kingdom, such a one would reveal a contradiction-in-will.

2) Next, suppose with Heribert Mühlen[18] that, since the Holy Spirit is the unity-bond of Father and Son ("One Person *in* Two [divine] Persons"), He can fittingly be designated as the "We" of the Trinity— that is, as the "We" constitutive of their intersubjective communion of life. Suppose, too, that this same personal "We" (the Third Person) is the missioned unity-bond between the divine Word and that humanity which both was hypostatically assumed in the virgin and is now incarnationally elevated throughout the entire human community. Then this Spirit (now "one Person *in* many [human] persons") constitutes the new saving koinonia which is the whole Christ. Jesus, glorified as Lord, employs his Mystical Body to call sinful individuals to conversion and to life at a human-divine level. Hence it seems most fitting that the Holy Spirit will again be "one Person in many persons," constituting the personal "We" that is the active source of the unity of Christians both with their Head and with each other. Since this Spirit of love cannot treasure any of Christ's redeemed communities any less than does Christ in his self-dedication to his bride,[19] the Loyalty of the Spirit must embrace each local Christian community, as well as today's world-wide body of those professing belief in Christ and that "universal Church" which stretches "from Abel, the just one, to the last of the elect."[20] Accordingly, when poured into the hearts of the faithful, this Spirit will instil within their *caritas* something of His own uniquely Personal, as well as communally Trinitarian, love for these koinonias whose unity and life He

[18] H. Mühlen, *Der Heilige Geist als Person* (Münster: Aschendorf, 1963) 100, 306–7; see also his *Una Mystica Persona* (Munich: F. Schöningh, 1964).

[19] Rev 3:9; Eph 5:25–27.

[20] Constitution on the Church, no. 2 (*Documents* 16).

constitutes (2:15). So, like this Spirit, we should love graced communities as such.

3) Our final musement arises when a person compares and contrasts both his own ideal self with his factually experienced self and this pair with other individuals and communities—with merely natural communities as well as genuinely loyal ones. Suppose, then, that none of the Three Persons of the Trinity can be "Himself" unless He freely gives Himself in love to the two other Persons and to Their shared life. Suppose, too, that human persons are constituted in the image of God as persons essentially related to others, even if essentially unique. Then a human person can find truest self-fulfilment only through a transcendent giving of himself to others.[21]

Yet toward this notion of such giving of oneself one experiences a certain ambivalence. This reveals in part one's actual self with its love-hate tendencies toward society and other individuals. To say the least, these ambivalent tendencies generate "turbulence" in the individual and in society. What, then, would loving another morally detached individual simply as such consist in? It would mean loving a person who is, like oneself, just as pulled apart by divergent tendencies and rendered just as acutely defensive against the demands of society. Hence to love only another morally detached individual simply as such is to engage in caprice, exclusion, and hopelessness; for such individualistic love has to be arbitrary in its selection of a beloved and can offer no hope of healing and integrating either onself or one's beloved or this "dangerous pair."[22] Nor does it offer hope of continuously avoiding unfair self-assertion.

However, the saving ambience of a genuinely loyal (graced) community may enter into such a couple and empower them to love each other in a transformed way. Then the above-mentioned wholehearted giving of onself to a genuine community with its openness to the universe of all minded beings becomes feasible indeed.

For one's truest self-fulfilment lies in that life-situation and growth-environment which both heals one's felt divisions and draws forth one's own potentials to the full. But one cannot even conceive of such a life-enriching situation and environment except in some ideal community of persons who know, love, and rejoice in one another and in their sharing of "one conscious spiritual whole of life" (1:406). Hence, by one's inmost self-ideal and one's quest for self-identity, as set within the context of finding oneself actually individualistic and in need of healing, one is directed from within to love that kind of community which heals and integrates oneself. In sum, our inmost nature directs us to love graced communities as such.

[21] See The Church in the Modern World, no. 24 (*Documents* 223).
[22] *HGC* 63.

CONCLUSION

We find, then, by exegesis of Paul's doctrine of love and by philosophical musements, that *caritas* directs us to love, besides individuals, graced communities as such. Some final words seem in order about our shift in the method of dealing with our question and about our pragmatic response to it.

Having neglected "the world of signs," most metaphysicians have attempted to base their positions on just one or two categories. For example, they may start from substance or process, or from reality and process taken as coultimate categories. Similarly, they may build upon the universal and/or the individual, upon the absolute and/or the relational, yet leave out the Spirit of sign-interpretation which brings both to unity. Experience shows how inadequate such positions are for generating a holistic view of reality (2:274–76). In the present essay I have replaced such category-based metaphysical thinking with the kind that benefits from a method of interpretive musement. For this I employed the life of interpretation. This kind of life process unites into community many minded beings: finite individual selves, communities of various rank, and the divine Spirit. My hope is that this method of interpretive musement, when based on genuine loyalty (and on grace), provides a more human way of philosophizing.

This shift in method, however, heightens the felt need for some guide in the unavoidable practical choices that mark everyday human living. I make no claim of having settled our question theoretically. But practically, our working hypothesis for directing life-preferences can become: act as if graced communities are real hyperpersonal realities that both love us and call for our loving loyalty. By moving into the future through decisions prompted by love for both kinds of reality—individual persons and Spirit-unified communities—we bring both into fuller presence and development. Pragmatically, we can act as if various beloved communities are actually loving, nurturing, fostering us, trusting our free creative responses to their guidance, and calling us to that kind of intelligently discerning loyalty that puts order into our love for other individuals and ourselves.

The practical exigence upon us, then, will be to return dedicated love and service—of course, to each Person in the Holy Trinity, to Christ as the human-divine Person, and to all individual persons we are privileged to live with, seen or unseen—but also to all the beloved communities giving us life. In ascending order, these will include all graced human families as such, humankind itself as graced and called by the Spirit of Christ, the Christian community baptized by Christ's Spirit into taking part in the divine life, the hypostatic community of the Second Person in the human nature of His past, present, and future selves and the holy Trinitarian Koinonia Itself. These communities challenge us to respond in faithfulness to them because their actually mixed life of deeds and ideals calls out: "Create us; make us more present or more real in your midst!" (2:428). If our deeds carry out this call, we will have found a pragmatic way both to acknowledge the Holy Spirit's presence and activity in such genuine community that touches our lives and to help heal, through atoning deeds, those nongenuine communities that afflict us and others. By responding this way, we will render the presence of the Spirit a perceptible reality for the people and communities that we in turn touch. We will also allow both our talents and shortcomings to become clay in the Potter's hands as He molds us into living signs of His loving Spirit.

Concerning justice, I view it as an aspect of human life that requires both ethico-religious and communally institutionalized dimensions in individuals and society. Experience shows that a focusing on just one or other "kind" of justice can often impede the process of human development. Instead, we need to integrate at least seven "kinds" of justice into one well-ordered "will to promote life." That is, we need to combine the traditional triad (of commutative + distributive + legal kinds of justice) with the more contemporary tetrad (of linguistic + "socially solid" + procedural + "history-and-hope-appreciative" kinds of justice)[23] even while remaining open to demands from some still uncharted kinds of justice. Because this multifaceted justice requires the integration of many dimensions, I view the process of radical ongoing conversion, in individuals and in communities, as an indispensable condition for promoting integral human justice. (Royce would call this the need for a transformation into a loving loyalty for humankind's Great Community.) For without such continuing conversion and discerningly loving loyalty to communities as such, individualistic loves become more disordered and the societal structures produced and fostered by them grow increasingly unjust.

My closing reflection concerns us Christians today. It arises from the contrast between Jesus' wholehearted commitment to his Father's kingdom and the seeming lack of commitment for graced communities in his present-day disciples' doctrine of the kingdom. That kingdom is, of course, both an eschatological reality and an ideal already partially

---

[23] Instances of these four contemporary kinds of justice may be found described in Paul VI's *Paths of the Church*, near close, John XXIII's *Peace on Earth* (New York: America, 1963; based on official Latin text of *AAS* 55, 257–304), John Rawls's *A Theory of Justice* (Cambridge, Mass.: Harvard, 1971), and H. Richard Niebuhr's *The Responsible Self* (New York: Harper & Row, 1963) respectively.

realized in our space-time world. This embodied foreshadowing of the kingdom comprises, besides individual members, both the various graced communities of humankind and the universal community of the Logos-Spirit sent to gather into unity all nations of history and all realms of minded beings. Jesus' reported directive, "Seek ye first the kingdom," has many meanings. Among these, might one be "Commit yourself wholeheartedly to graced communities as embodiments of the kingdom, as part of his body to be lovingly fostered, sacrificed for, and beautified, the way Christ loves his Church"?[24]

[24] This essay points to Josiah Royce as a seminal North American philosopher of community. That pointing has since been intensified by the publication of John Clendenning's long-awaited *The Life and Thought of Josiah Royce* (Madison: University of Wisconsin Press, 1985).

J. J. Mueller

Appreciative Awareness: The Feeling-Dimension in Religious Experience

J. J. Mueller, S.J., is associate professor of historical and systematic theology at St. Louis University. His main area of interest is theology and culture, especially in the North American theological context. He is the author of *Faith and Appreciative Awareness* and *What Are Theologians Saying about Theological Method?*

RELIGIOUS EXPERIENCE is the term which describes the encounter between the human person and God. The sensations, feelings, emotions, mind, and spirit are the arenas which mediate the experience to consciousness. Knowledge results which is at the same time both clear and unclear. Reason may come to know clearly the distinction between the economic and immanent Trinity, but the heart recognizes the triune presence. The experience always remains richer than knowledge. Like a lit candle placed in the center of a dark room, the area close to the flame is clear and details are seen. But as one looks to the more remote areas of the room, the light cannot penetrate the darkness, details become obscure, and only large objects are discernible. The obscured objects remain no less real than the illuminated ones.

The challenge confronting theology is the person who seeks to understand faith in the world today and who wants faith to issue into a deeper love of God. Therefore the question is not whether God manifests Himself to me in experience but how I communicate with Him. This chapter will examine the manner in which the person in the feeling-dimension of religious experience communicates with God. I am primarily concerned, then, with the knowledge of the heart. Bernard E. Meland calls it "appreciative knowledge."

Appreciative knowledge is best described by the analogy to art. In this aesthetic mode the feelings rather than logic lead the individual in the encounter. Thus the person cannot be a viewer but becomes a participant on the feeling-dimension. The analogy does not focus upon the relationship of creating but of appreciating art. The act of appreciating implies an interaction between the person and an "other" which forms a context of relationships. Appreciative knowledge, then, depends upon recognition, a discernment of sorts, that perceives what the feelings convey in relationship with another, whether the other is an El Greco painting, music by Beethoven, or sculpture by Rodin. Hence the art object interacts

121

with the feelings and communicates through them on the appreciative dimension.

Appreciative knowledge extends beyond the art analogy—which is often limited to fine arts—to include the feeling-dimension as a way of living towards all creation. Thus the appreciative dimension indicates a mode of being in the world. Much of our daily living is saturated by appreciative knowledge: how we feel about the day when we wake up, how we feel about issues whether political, ethical, or personal, and how we feel about ourselves. One recognizes a familiar face, a friendly voice, a loving embrace. Like two people falling in love, appreciative knowledge grows with each passing day, and words like tips of icebergs only hint at the depths involved. This unspoken, nonverbal, yet expressed reality communicates appreciative knowledge on the feeling-dimension with the result that one knows life in another way. By the same process one also knows God.

While systematic theologians generally acknowledge the place of the feeling-dimension in religious experience, few develop how God employs this dimension to communicate Himself to us. Though David Tracy accepts common human experience and language as indispensable for his theological method, his preferences are the ontological truth-claims of experience.[1] Bernard Lonergan's comprehensive method in theology examines the multileveled conversion of the Christian. Lonergan wrote his book with a threefold conversion (intellectual, moral, religious) and only recently added a fourth, which now needs development: affective conversion.[2] Karl Rahner's incarnational theology invites an examination of the feeling-dimension as a means of God's communication to the individual, but he lacks a theory of affectivity for individual religious experience and also seems unable to situate the individual adequately within a larger social context.[3] Developing out of Rahner's theology, yet reacting to limitations, Johannes Metz and the liberation theologians included the cultural context as a primary source for theology and employed socioeconomic and political analyses.[4] While liberation theo-

---

[1] D. Tracy, *Blessed Rage for Order* (New York: Seabury, 1975) 52–56.

[2] B. J. F. Lonergan, *Method in Theology* (New York: Herder & Herder, 1972) 283–84.

[3] One example from the extensive Rahner corpus is *Foundations of Christian Faith* (New York: Seabury, 1978) 138–76. He prefers the category "history" to culture, and his main concern is revelation and knowledge, God's freedom and human freedom forming a unity so that salvation history and human history are coextensive. His popular and devotional works contain the feeling-dimension but without any integration with his theological work. W. Dych's presentation of Rahner's themes is helpful: "Theology in a New Key," in *A World of Grace*, ed. L. O'Donovan (New York: Seabury, 1980) 1–17.

[4] J.-B. Metz, *Faith in History and Society* (New York: Seabury, 1980), elaborates a "new political theology" (ix) for fundamental theology. His use of history as a context for self-analysis capitalizes on memory as the medium by which reason becomes practical as

logians include the feeling-dimension, pain and suffering so override every other feeling that they preclude any other option, with the result that these theologians have so far been unable to provide a well-rounded analysis of religious experience. Edward Schillebeeckx' theology of "mediated immediacy" provides a more positive context than liberation theology for listening to God (e.g., the discovery of penicillin as a moment of God's grace) and also takes the feeling-dimension as integral to theology with suffering as the starting point.[5] His main concern is the inculturation of Scripture both in the first century and today, not religious experience as a way of knowing God. Complementing the work and direction of these theologians, yet providing an analysis of the feeling-dimension lacking in each of these, Meland provides a systematic theology from the perspective of appreciative knowledge.

Meland is a cultural theologian who contributes an examination of the feeling-dimension of the believer. His theological vision develops from his Anglo-American tradition, especially the philosophical insights of William James and Alfred North Whitehead. In *The Analogical Imagination* David Tracy boldly states: "It might be noted that, in the Anglo-American empirical (not empiricist) tradition, Meland's work represents the major example of the art-religion analogy."[6] Meland's sensitivity to the dynamics of a technological age coming about in the United States offered him the possibility of an insightful theology far ahead of its time that is today a renewable source of insights for religious experience.

Who is Bernard Meland? What is his appreciative knowledge? What does it offer to the current state of theology? My article will answer these three questions. I will begin with Meland's intellectual journey as one paradigm that perhaps many people share; explore his key theological insight of appreciative consciousness and its turning into a skilled responsive awareness; show how appreciative awareness fits within a theology and is interrelated with faith; examine the wider context of culture as the context for faith; and apply his insights to the pastoral problem of prayer.

MELAND'S INTELLECTUAL JOURNEY

It seems fitting that from Meland's apartment window in Chicago he looked over the Museum of Science and Industry. Meland lived the advent

---

freedom. For a less formal and more evocative presentation, see Metz, *The Emergent Church* (New York: Crossroad, 1981). As for liberation theologians, many commonly express what E. Dussel articulates: "If we want to train people, we send them to Europe.... When they come back, they are completely lost in Latin America.... They are Frenchified, Germanized, or otherwise alienated" (*History and the Theology of Liberation* [Maryknoll, N.Y.: Orbis, 1976] 18).

[5] E. Schillebeeckx, *Christ* (New York: Seabury, 1980) 724–31.

[6] D. Tracy, *The Analogical Imagination* (New York: Crossroad, 1981) 219, n. 8.

of new science and industry while developing a profound sensitivity to the feeling-dimension of the experience of the modern world. It was the dialectic of science and art, rational and irrational, thinking and feeling, from which his contribution emerged.

Meland's intellectual journey begins from the early-twentieth-century upheaval and the creative group that formed the "Chicago School."[7] The first 25 years of this century at Chicago were dominated by Dewey's influence, where function took precedence over metaphysical reality. Empirical disciplines, encouraged by science, held the upper hand. Theologically, doctrine was considered as derived from a specific need. Not until the 1920's did this instrumentation achieve a depth and awareness consolidated by Gerald Birney Smith and Henry Nelson Wieman. Both were aided by the process cosmology of Alfred North Whitehead and William James's radical empiricism.

G. B. Smith was Meland's mentor and was a catalyst at a timely stage of Meland's intellectual development. It was Smith who suggested that religious response was nearer to the arts than science. Smith's untimely death in 1929, only one week after approving Meland's Ph.D. thesis, left Meland with a direction but not the road to travel.

Henry Nelson Wieman was brought to the Chicago campus in 1926 to explain the new insights of Alfred North Whitehead. That lecture ignited a small fire that burned for decades.[8] Wieman was subsequently hired by the university and helped forge its direction. When Meland returned to the University of Chicago in 1946 to teach, he became a close colleague of Wieman.

Wieman, who deserves more attention than he has received for his distinctive approach to process/relational theology, pursued an empirical path along the model of scientific objectivity. His personal penchant for clarity led him to ask whether or not he should move entirely to a scientific model of truth. While in conversation with Meland, Wieman decided on the scientific model. At that moment Meland realized that another option was called for along the lines of an artistic model.

Trained as he had been in the empirical methodology of the early Chicago School, yet nurtured by his own aesthetic developments throughout the 1930's and 1940's,[9] Meland realized that conceptual clarity was

[7] Meland is considered one of the finest historians of the Chicago School; see his "Introduction: The Empirical Tradition in Theology at Chicago," in *The Future of Empirical Theology*, ed. B. Meland (Chicago: University of Chicago, 1969) 1–62. For a fine presentation of his early development, see L. Axel, "The Root and Form of Meland's Elementalism," *Journal of Religion* 60 (1980) 472–90.

[8] For an account of the impact of this lecture for the Univ. of Chicago faculty, see Meland, *The Realities of Faith* (New York: Oxford University, 1962) 109–11.

[9] One important development was Meland's study in Europe in the 1930's under Rudolph

not necessarily clearer truth. Truth often defied rational clarity and belonged to the "wisdom of the body." His road became clear. Experience remained the richer concept which needed examination on the feeling-dimension. Meland's intellectual and aesthetic development coalesced at this time to form his concept of the appreciative consciousness, which unified his vision and gave birth to his major theological achievement, the trilogy: *Faith and Culture* (1953), *The Realities of Faith: The Revolution in Cultural Forms* (1962), *Fallible Forms and Symbols: Discourses on Method for a Theology of Culture* (1976). In this trilogy he expressed his systematic theology and etched the lines of this theological vision bolstered by the appreciative consciousness.

Meland has an image that summarizes his theological vision and expresses rather well the dimension that he probes. Reflecting upon his own theological vision, he remembered the poet-churchman John Donne's statement "No man is an island." Meland mused: "Might he not better have said 'Every man is an island' but islands are not what they appeared to be: isolated bodies of land, for if one presses beneath the surface of the water one will come upon a land base that unites these individual bodies of land."[10] Meland is a theologian who quests for the sense of the wholeness in life. While some see only parts, he penetrates to the interconnected whole. Persons, events, experiences, and meaning are not isolated islands standing alone in the ocean. Press beneath the surface of one's superficial perceptions and one finds a connectedness which discloses a united, intertwined, and web-like structure of reality. Meland challenges the person not only to think but also to feel the texture of this reality. Thus thinking and feeling go together. *How* they go together is the work of the appreciative awareness.

Finally, Meland has made some clear choices that should be expected to appear in the treatment of a topic: he is optimistic rather than pessimistic, positive rather than negative, intuitive rather than logical, poetic rather than scientific. His work does leave open possible developments in other directions.

THE APPRECIATIVE CONSCIOUSNESS

While Meland was publishing the first volume of his trilogy in 1953, he simultaneously published a book on higher education with a significant chapter entitled "The Appreciative Consciousness."[11] Although he pre-

---

Otto. He was also exposed to the Christian art and architecture of Europe, which nourished his aesthetic sensitivity.

[10] Meland, *Realities of Faith* 231.

[11] Meland, *Higher Education and the Human Spirit* (Chicago: University of Chicago, 1953).

sents cryptic explanations of the appreciative consciousness throughout his theological writings, he never repeats the in-depth explanation contained in this seminal article.[12] The result is that appreciative consciousness can be overlooked.[13]

Meland defines the appreciative consciousness in both a comparative and a descriptive way. The comparative definition is in polite opposition to both the rational and the moral consciousness. Beginning with Greek thought, the Western mind emphasized the role of reason-as-analysis. Reason's purpose is conceptual clarification. This process distills experience into concepts. Its concepts are not the realities known. There is no one-to-one correspondence between a clarified concept and the reality conveyed. The moral consciousness, on the other hand, is an organizing principle which gathers together, sifts, and structures the individual's knowledge through moral obligation, which in turn commands action. Action can be correlated with thought as a legitimate theological category of experience. Kant is one who explained this mode and gave it modern support.

Beginning with William James and Henri Bergson and culminating in Whitehead, a third mode of consciousness received solid philosophical underpinning: the appreciative consciousness. Meland describes this mode as "a regulative principle in thought which as an orientation of the mind makes for a maximum degree of receptivity to the datum under consideration on the principle that what is given may be more than one thinks."[14] Thus there is another mode of consciousness along with the rational and the moral consciousness which operates on a feeling, perceptive, and appreciative level in experience. With this mode, categories at hand fail to exhaust the meaning of the datum, and what is being attended to in experience cannot be reduced to some structure already known and defined. This mode of consciousness entails an "intellectual humility" to what one knows and clarifies, a "wonder" toward reality, "reverence," or simply "open awareness." Whatever one prefers to call it, such an attitude is essential to the orientation of the mind.

[12] For a brief overview of Meland's works, see C. Williamson, "Bernard E. Meland: What Kind of Theologian?" *Journal of Religion* 60 (1980) 369–90. Williamson mentions an interesting story: at a fall 1978 meeting of the American Theological Society (Midwest division), the participants were each convinced that none of the others rightly interpreted Meland. My own research indicates that the appreciative consciousness is the skeleton key to Meland scholarship which unlocks the various interpretations.

[13] I believe the lack of attention to this development is an important oversight in Meland scholarship. Reintroducing the explanation of the appreciative consciousness as foundational to this theology would clarify many elements. I have tried to do this in my *Faith and Appreciative Awareness* (Washington, D.C.: University Press of America, 1981).

[14] *Higher Education* 63; also Mueller, *Faith* 13–23, for a more complete explanation.

Meland wrote this article in 1953. Since then, particularly in the 1970's, the mode of appreciative consciousness, though not referred to as such, has become increasingly recognized as integral to human experience. Feeling, valuations, aesthetics, and the "irrational" dimensions of the psyche receive greater acceptance today in the way we live and how we think of ourselves.

The widespread use of appreciative consciousness can be illustrated through recent discoveries in medicine. From work on epileptic conditions, the "split-brain" analysis emerged. Basically, the human brain is divided into two halves which are connected at the center of the cerebral cavity by a tissue. When the two halves are separated surgically (to aid an epileptic for example), the response is remarkable. Generally speaking, the left side of our brain perceives the world in a logical and rational way. The left creates concepts of causality. The right side is "irrational" and perceives whole patterns. When each hemisphere is tested, it is the left brain which remembers how to speak and use words which the right brain cannot. However, the right brain remembers the lyrics of songs. The left side tends to ask questions of our sensory input; the right tends to accept it.[15] In Meland the rational consciousness aproximates the left side, the appreciative consciousness the right side. Meland spotted, and I think correctly, that the cultural stress on reason had forsaken another important element in human knowing and then attempted to correct it. Meland's fundamental insight maintains that the "irrational" dimension is a form of knowing. He joins William James in affirming that to make use of this form of knowing one need not empty oneself into subjectivism, emotivism, or pietism, as if one were an island untouched by challenge, science, or common agreement.

At this point Meland's vocabulary seems more reminiscent of James's than Whitehead's.[16] James's colorful and evocative vocabulary speaks of "perception," "stream of consciousness," "the doctrine of the fringe of consciousness," the "more" of reality, and "feeling of tendency." James's "fringe of consciousness" is particularly expressive of the appreciative mode, for it calls attention to areas that are not clearly focused, separated

[15] For a fascinating popular presentation of rational consciousness in physics and its gradual move toward a more appreciative consciousness, see G. Zukav, *The Dancing Wu Li Masters: An Overview of the New Physics* (New York: Morrow, 1979). For a technical explanation, see B. Kolb and I. Whishaw, *Fundamentals of Human Neuropsychology* (San Francisco: Freeman, 1980).

[16] Meland has been seen by some as more "Jamesian" than "Whiteheadian"; cf. D. Tracy, *Blessed Rage for Order* 202. This interpretation, perhaps based on language similarities, is not substantively correct, for Meland insists on the American tradition of philosophers from James through Whitehead as part of the same process tradition. Cf. Meland's review of C. Eisendrath's *The Unifying Moment* in *Process Studies* no. 3 (1973) 285-90.

out, or distilled, yet form parts of the thicker, richer wholeness. Rational consciousness provides the reflective focus of the mind toward reality, rendering its aspects reflectively discriminated. James understood the mind in the large sense as the center of the entire person, including sensations and feelings. Reality conveyed a feeling tone, or a "more" than what can be comprehended, a dimension "thicker" than what can be distilled. Meland designates this dimension as "depth."

We build our lives upon appreciative knowledge. When I say that I played a hunch, felt right about someone, felt something was wrong, or had an intuition, I have opened myself to the "more" of reality and correctly perceived a flow of events. An expression like "When you're hot, you're hot" describes an athlete, a musician, a speaker, or a comedian moving correctly with the flow of events in such a way that the person is interwoven with an event larger than himself or herself. Athletes are aware of this creative state and struggle to achieve it. The author and athlete Arthur Ashe calls it "the zone" which athletes strive for. Bjorn Borg describes it as a feeling, completely conscious, of being able to do anything with a tennis racket, and so he attempts shots that no one has done and he knows he will succeed. Tony Dorsett, the Dallas Cowboy running back, says he can feel tacklers coming at him from the blind side and he cuts in another direction. The result is that two would-be tacklers smash into each other. People who depend upon appreciative knowledge feel the flow of events from the inside. Creativity often results and they do things seemingly beyond themselves. The effect is a relational unity and the player becomes the play, the dancer becomes the dance, the musician becomes the music.

Meland offers examples of appreciative consciousness. One is the appreciation of the values in another culture, e.g., the peasants in Mexico when seen by a United States tourist. Culturally, the peasants do not seem to measure up to the technological standards of a U.S. culture. The "ugly American" syndrome sets in and the tourist becomes cynical about the peasants' backwardness, lack of sophistication in tools and life style, and lack of industriousness. Their reality of the situation is that different values are at work that cannot be univocally judged by one culture's mind-set. Islands may not be what they appear. Simplicity, down-to-earthness, a slower pace of life are foreign to the American tourist but no less valid. Unless a tourist "feels into" the new situation with other values and appreciates reality experienced in different ways, the "enlightened" rational reply may be a debunking cynicism.

In another example, a small town's life could be told by a sociologist or a historian. Each would present important truths about the town. But the best chronicler might be the novelist who can give a feeling for the people's triumphs, struggles, and setbacks to allow an appreciation of their values and to convey their world from the inside. In both examples the appreciative consciousness penetrates an important and needed truth of reality.

APPRECIATIVE AWARENESS

When a person visits an art gallery and stands in front of a painting, he or she engages in a relationship with the painting whereby the painting communicates on the feeling level. No words are spoken but a communication occurs. The person may feel delighted, disgusted, attracted, or repelled. It is not enough to experience the feelings. One also determines whether this painting of itself has a message. If it does, do I correctly interpret the meaning? People who have honed their skills through the history of art, knowledge of color, line, texture, composition, etc., develop their critical ability to correctly interpret the painting. We say that these people have an appreciation for painting. If I do not have an appreciation for painting, or at least only a small appreciation, I might talk with my expert friend about how to understand line, color, etc. The language we use discloses what the painting means in the hope that I can then look at this painting with new appreciation. My analysis hones my skill to correctly interpret the painting. The art historian Jane Dillenberger puts this extremely well:

> In making an analysis of painting or sculpture, we are compelled to verbalize that for which there is no verbal counterpart. Language must be probing and pointing rather than definitive. Most important of all, the language must focus on the work of art itself, rather than on ideas about the work of art. It must compel the reader to become a viewer.[17]

The appreciative awareness is a term I use to indicate the turning of the appreciative consciousness or knowledge into a skill. Meland does not distinguish the two so radically, but I think that for clarity's sake it is important to retain the difference.

Meland knows the danger of subjectivism as well as of objectivism. The appreciative dimension is more prone to subjectivism. Therefore, in a significant epistemological move, he suggests the skill of appreciative awareness as a corrective measure situated in the gap between subjectivism and objectivism. This three-step methodological move allows the "reader to become a viewer."

1) If the starting point of the appreciative consciousness is the mystery

[17] Jane Dillenberger, *Secular Art with Sacred Themes* (New York: Abingdon, 1969) 12. For Meland's own acceptance and assessment of Dillenberger's quotation as correctly summarizing his own approach, cf. Mueller, *Faith* x–xi.

of what is given in existence, e.g., a sunset or another person, then the
first act by the individual is of opened awareness. The rich fulness of the
event is allowed to disclose or declare itself without preconceived premises. Nor does one encounter the event with instrumental or functional
purposes. Receptiveness to the other becomes the initial conscious awareness. The attitude characteristic of this first step is wonder.

Moving out of the art analogy to a more comprehensive example, when
I am introduced to someone at a social gathering, I do not see this person
as "just another hand to be shaken." If I do, I have preconceived premises
and I am not allowing the other person to disclose himself or herself.
Receptiveness characterized by wonder is the initial presupposition to
allow the other to communicate with me.

Without this first step, there would be no Einsteinian theory of
relativity, no Rubik cube, no prayer of praise, no ritual response. Novel
and creative advance would vanish. Even our perception of God would
be confined to the defined areas of life, and then our perception would
not be God but an idol less than God.

2) The second step is identification. Once the person opens toward the
other, a reciprocal relationship occurs. The person and the event are
caught up together and two channels form. One channel funnels the data
into conscious experience which takes the form of symbolic representa-
tions. "Symbolization" is the procedure of creating meaning and of
interrelating meanings through communicable symbols.[18] For example,
once a person has been introduced to another, the process of interrelating
to the other through normal social amenities like "Where are you from?",
"What do you do?", etc., is a conscious attempt to symbolize the willingness to know another. Each question is cued by the preceding answer,
which leads to a process of getting to know another.

The other channel shares the feeling-context, not simply the cognitive
interaction. This feeling-context signifies more than what James and
Bergson talked about as inner knowledge by acquaintance, for it extends
beyond the subjective act of feeling and penetrates the event in such a
way that the individual and reality, the subjective and objective, the "I"
and the "it" find their common ground.[19] It thereby avoids the subjectiv-
istic tendencies by giving attention to the context itself as informing the
individual. In talking with another person, I begin to feel the direction
the conversation is going, whether I like this person initially, and whether
he or she likes me. By the tone in the voice, the gesture of the hand, the
movement of the eyes, more is communicated to me that I can distill out.
My feeling is that a moment of trust on both sides has been established

---

[18] Meland, *Faith and Culture* (New York: Oxford University, 1953) 140.
[19] Meland, *Higher Education* 65.

and confirmed which allows for a developing openness toward the other.

The context itself discloses a connectedness which is referred to in other areas as gestalt, web, and historical situation. Without attention to the felt texture of the context, the person simply feels his or her own feelings and projects them onto others. The characteristic attitude of this second step is empathy, which is the ability to share another's feelings.

3) The third step of appreciative awareness is discrimination. Though analytical, it does not extricate the datum from its context, for to do so would be to overreach rational boundaries for the sake of false certainty and clarity. The assumption which directs the appreciative awareness is that an event is never properly known apart from its context. Appreciative awareness offers the kind of knowledge obtained by studying an elephant in its natural habitat in Africa rather than in a zoo. When two people meet, for instance, they are conditioned by their historical environment: at a festival, not a funeral; in 1983, not 1783, etc.

Discrimination analyzes the datum and differentiates its particular features, allowing the rational consciousness to operate in its own realm. Dissection is important to bring out the various components in a given area of knowledge (e.g., line, color, shape, in·painting), but the components must be reassembled so that the integrity of the whole is not lost. Hence one must return to appreciate the painting again. Here Meland encourages critical reasoning and thereby avoids the tendency to subjectivism.[20] Perceptiveness, as James emphasized, becomes important because it attunes the person on all levels like an antenna to the dimension of depth. The rational mode helps direct the appreciative skill. Critical abilities of judgment and decision are not canceled out; rather they are brought into correct and critical relation with the individual and the event in one context. At a gathering of people, I might walk away for a few moments and realize that I have met 75 people and I didn't like the last person because I am tired—"my feelings cannot feel." It is not the other person but my own limits which get in the way. Discrimination of my feelings tells me that I am not this way normally.

This third step separates Meland from subjectivists because reason has a place and a critical activity. He therefore stands fast in the liberal theological tradition in North America where critical thinking is not opposed to faith. Using the insights from sociology, psychology, physics, etc., and the contribution they make to theology, he finds an integral

[20] Meland has remained with an empirical investigation of the appreciative consciousness. Those who develop the rational consciousness such as Lonergan, and the truth claims of ontology such as Tracy, became important dialogue partners to complete Meland's use of rational consciousness. Also, the moral consciousness does not receive much treatment from Meland. Liberation theologians, with their emphasis upon praxis as the starting point of theology, would enhance the moral dimension and extend Meland's work.

place for the appreciative consciousness correlated with the rational consciousness.

The method just described should not be exclusively identified with the aesthetic and poetic temperament. The use of the feeling-dimension through the skill of the appreciative awareness is open to nonpoetic temperaments: what aesthetics is to appreciative consciousness, logic is to rational consciousness. Neither logic nor aesthetics totally defines the awareness, but each does suggest and intimate the characteristics of its appropriate consciousness.

A further characteristic which separates Meland from epistemologists and aesthetes is the spiritual force of faith, which opens the person to God's manifestation of Himself. Meland uses appreciative awareness to probe and penetrate the meaning of reality from a faith context. From religious experience grounded in appreciative consciousness, skilled by appreciative awareness, and focused by faith, Meland generates his systematic theology.

APPRECIATIVE AWARENESS AND FAITH

The nourishing relationship between faith and the appreciative awareness becomes clearer when faith is examined. Without reference to the religious dimension, faith implies a basic trust. For example, two people who love one another marry each other in committed trust. With the inclusion of the religious dimension, faith becomes a trust in God. Although God manifests Himself through mediated reality, He underlies it and extends Himself beyond the total grasp of reasoning mind (e.g., Why do I love my spouse?). The mind, heart, feelings, and spirit possess a knowledge of their own, and together they manifest the immensity of God, but even they cannot envelop Him—God envelops us. Through faith in God, marriage then becomes matrimony. God comes to us as "a goodness not our own" that we experience on the feeling-dimension.[21] However, God is no less present even when the mind cannot pierce the cloud of unknowing or consciously advert to His presence.

Meland's basic analogue for faith is energy. Rather than focusing upon the moment of first conversion, his theology explores the continued involvement that faith entails. Faith expresses a relationship of encounter that bestows a redemptive energy whereby the person centers his or her life in God. Thus faith bestows a power of its own which might better be described as an empowerment. Meland expresses this empowering

---

[21] Meland prefers the designation of the experience of God as "a goodness not our own" throughout his work. For reasons that I present later in this article, this designation is too modest for the richness of religious experience. In addition, I believe a developmental model of religious conversion such as Lonergan's in *Method* or Tracy's in *Blessed Rage for Order* would enhance Meland's theology.

faith as "social, psychical, and redemptive energy within individual human beings, within corporate action among groups, within the culture, expressing this grace and judgment of relationships in terms of the resources that heal and redeem our ways."[22] For example, a married man lives with and in the love relationship of his wife and becomes empowered by the relationship as a source of energy for his living. Love becomes the living context which comes as both freely given (graciousness) and a commitment (judgment) to live by.

Meland prefers to de-emphasize faith as belief in a set of facts or doctrines in order to emphasize its vital, living, dynamic, and empowering quality. Faith energizes the way I treat people, where I go, and what I do. At the same time, Meland emphasizes God's freely giving of Himself in the structures of human living (e.g., a human encounter, a sunset, a walk, religious ritual) which are historically and culturally conditioned. Meland calls this context the "structure of experience." Like the air we breathe, God comes in many ways through the structured events of the past which push forward toward the future but are always experienced as present.[23]

While appreciative awareness and faith work together, care must be taken not to collapse one into the other and thereby secularize faith to a human skill or supernaturalize awareness to a type of gnosticism. Of the several possible avenues of approach, let me develop one which best fits the line of approach of this article.[24]

The difference between appreciative awareness and faith is the final orientation of each, or the difference between knowledge and love. Appreciative awareness moves toward knowledge as exemplified in the third step (discrimination). Thus the potential exists for self-improvement in the appreciative mode. For example, I might see my art-historian friend for a history of the painting. Or I might call upon the novelist to convey a "feeling into" the social situation of the small town that the analyst could not do.

Faith, however, orients the person to love. God initiates an encounter with the individual which is experienced as grace and judgment. If the person believes, then the whole person becomes committed in the act of faith. Although reason plays an important part, the conversion is not merely intellectual. While God is the goal of faith, He is not grasped immediately and visibly in the same way that another individual is who walks into my room and closes the door. God is mediated to me through

[22] Meland, *Fallible Forms and Symbols* (Philadelphia: Fortress, 1976) 27.

[23] For a fuller treatment, see Mueller, *Faith* 35–54.

[24] In Mueller, *ibid.* 111–24, three ways of distinguishing faith and appreciative awareness are developed: by their intentionality, by method, and by the dimension of spirit they convey.

my self, others, events. Affectively, God is experienced "as a goodness not our own" which remains other than myself. The rich self-communication of God as goodness manifests Him at the same time as graciousness and judgment (freely offered for acceptance or rejection) and is experientially realized also as a forgiveness in the sense that sins are no longer the point of life but God is. It is not enough to know one is a sinner; one must also live toward God. Faith opens us to God. The encounter with God that is expressed empirically by goodness requires a response in kind, i.e., our goodness. Goodness is not an intellectual understanding but a totally involving relationship. Two centers of freedom meet and become involved when the individual accepts the initiating goodness offered by God. Although Meland prefers the general expression of goodness, I prefer the more specific expression of love from which goodness flows. Hence God is experienced more specifically as "a love not our own" where God's self-communication is not only good but essentially an act also of love. The response on my part calls for the return in kind which is love. Thus faith is the return of my love to God who has first loved me. This relationship empowers me to live my life toward ever-greater involvement with God in love.

The movement toward love is not simply described as two people entering into an I-thou relationship like two friends or lovers. The movement by God toward the person is a relation that is total, faithful to the end, and requires a similar response by the individual. The special characteristic of this relationship is expressed by the word "covenant." The social aspect of the covenant relation includes others who become my neighbors as brother and sister, hence a "we" relationship as well. Most fundamentally, I am and remain an individual-in-community. The knowledge which results from love is real knowledge of the appreciative kind, born and bred in love, which testifies to a depth so that "islands are not what they appear to be."

Thus faith ultimately brings the appreciative consciousness to the service of love. The faith relationship with God uses the appreciative skills to find Him present manifesting Himself in daily events. Ordinary love becomes extraordinary, and symbols become sacraments. At the same time, love requires the service of the appreciative consciousness to bring nurture and sensitivity to the love relationship on the feeling-dimension as exhibited in prayer, worship, ritual, and symbol. The appreciative consciousness, constantly honed by reflection, generates in everyday life a greater harmonious love with God. Thus appreciative awareness and faith do not lose their proper identities. By working together, they open the feeling-dimension of religious experience to God's communing love.

APPRECIATIVE AWARENESS AND CULTURE

One of the components which make up an event within which the faith experience of God is mediated is culture. The person relates to the context of culture also through the appreciative consciousness guided by faith. For Meland, culture is a key concept: "Culture connotes the total complex of human growth that has occurred within any clearly defined orbit of human association, expressing its prevailing sentiment, style, and way of life."[25] In a slightly different definition oriented toward the human person, he says: "Culture, in short, is the corporate, qualitative manifestation of the human psyche expressed through a community at any given level of civilization."[26] Civilization is the current stage of a culture (e.g., technological civilization instead of agrarian) and culture carries the values of many civilizations. The carriers of culture are humanly made and therefore fallible forms and symbols (e.g., institutions, political structures, art, furniture, tools, clothing, etc.). The believer always lives in a given cultural context and relates to God through the medium of religious experience, which finds expression both in thought (*logos*) and symbol (*mythos*). Cathedrals, religious art, customs, rituals, and devotions are a few of the fallible forms and symbols which act as mediums for the encounter with God. Profound religious conversions and continual nourishment take place through these inculturated forms. The appreciative consciousness allows one to encounter God speaking through various times and places.

Meland has deliberately attacked the misleadingly clear boundary lines between the world as profane and the Church as sacred, between where God cannot and can be. Such humanly drawn lines restrict God's presence in life, as if God is only present inside the Church. In the context of God's creation as good, Meland's holistic approach searches for God's presence wherever God wishes to manifest Himself. The emphasis is upon the human person's openness to listen to God under God's conditions whatever they be. If faith is not constantly attuned to the changes occurring anew, it loses much of its vitality both in awareness of cultural relationships and responses to them (e.g., changes in role identities of men and women, political decisions of national and internal policies, the use of authority and power, use of material goods and comforts, etc.). Culture can misleadingly be looked upon as an enemy from the perspective of secularism that states God cannot dwell there. Meland is not willing to accept such a dire conclusion because it both reduces God to human proportion and ultimately leaves the human person and community forsaken. God does not forsake us but continues to draw us with our culture to Himself through the creative passage.

[25] *Fallible Forms* 155.   [26] *Realities of Faith* 308.

APPRECIATIVE AWARENESS AND CREATIVE PASSAGE

Each event, called the structure of experience, is open to creative and loving possibilities which involve myself and God. Depth describes this feeling-dimension which underpins our lives and opens us to the beckoning lure of God experienced as goodness, beauty, and love. Since God is involved in the structure of experience in a creative way, Meland prefers to identify God's interacting presence through the term "creative passage." He describes it as "the basic characterization of existences as it applies to all life, to all people, to all cultures."[27] The creative passage is his most comprehensive designation of all reality.

As Meland understands it, the dimension of depth in the creative passage goes beyond surface perceptions. He categorizes three general ways which he refers to as "witnesses of faith" by which we gather up depth in Western history: cultus, culture, and the individual.[28] While Meland will only speak within his own Western history, his categories certainly transcend it. The cultus refers to the tradition of those who believe and the symbols carried from the past in both its thought and feeling (e.g., the Christian religion, the Jewish religion). Culture refers to the events of belief which have continued into the present, especially as these are located in religious art, cathedrals, furnishings, government, and social behavior. The individual refers to the personal testimonies from the past and present (e.g., saints, friends, family) and, above all, includes my own personal story. When these three witness to the Christian revelation, they give rise to "a complex of symbols and signs, expressed or anticipated, which contribute to a sense of orientation and familiarity in one's mode of existence."[29] By means of the appreciative awareness, each cluster of relationships witnesses to God's love through faith.

In the actual experience of God, since God is mediated through the creative passage by His own initiation but dependent upon human receptivity, the appreciative awareness functions much as a lens in aiding faith to perceive what is there. Faith becomes focused through the appreciative awareness.

Here again it is important to determine the difference between faith and appreciative awareness, because experience needs to be tested to discover whether it is truly from God. This is the problem of discernment, which extends beyond this article. In general, it can be said that whatever knowledge we have about God and the way He communicates is extremely important. While God can be neither totally isolated by one human

---

[27] *Fallible Forms* xiii. A helpful glossary of Meland's terms is in Mueller, *Faith* 135–38.
[28] For a fuller treatment in Meland, see Mueller, *Faith* 55–83.
[29] *Fallible Forms* 173.

tradition nor contained within it, the Christian tradition offers an unparalleled revelation in Jesus the Christ. This tradition is a legacy which includes everything touched by the Christian experience: cultus, culture, and individual. The constant and privileged norm of identification within the Christian experience is Jesus the Christ, who is the visible presence of the invisible God. For Meland, since Jesus is the aperture for the representation of Christian tradition, he is the key for the identification of God in the creative passage for each generation. Thus revelation of God in Jesus complements the empirical search for God in religious experience.

Faith in God cannot stand still; it must develop. As knowledge grows from mutual love, faith depends to some extent upon the growth which the appreciative awareness provides. For example, as an individual-in-community, I experience a need to express my personal and corporate faith on the feeling-dimension in ritual, symbol, and prayer. Without the appreciative consciousness, faith loses much of its vitality both in awareness and in response; a truncated rational response or moral action masquerades as religious experience and declares: "Islands are what they appear to be."

APPRECIATIVE PRAYER

Meland's theological framework is now in place. Once the foundation of appreciative consciousness is laid and the blueprint of appreciative awareness drawn, the main pillars of faith, culture, and creative passage are set. To finish the construction, one must move from talk about theology to doing theology; one must move from spectator to participant. While I find his seminal insights capable of enriching many pastoral concerns, let me take the current problematic of prayer as one example where I think his theology can be helpful.

While not everyone formally theologizes, nearly everyone does pray at some time (e.g., a moment of praise, thanksgiving, tragedy, sorrow). Prayer is an integral part of religious experience in Christian and non-Christian traditions. Whether done in private or in common, it is a deeply human experience. For the Christian, it is a necessary dimension of faith. Both saints and sinners, the converted and unconverted, the found and the lost pray. The perennial problem is praying itself, which might be expressed in the question "How do I pray?" The "how" question is action-oriented and springs appropriately from the moral consciousness. However, one must also know what one is doing, and consequently the "what" question springs somewhat more from the rational consciousness. Both questions interpenetrate each other, because prayer both springs from experience and returns to it to form further experience itself. Nevertheless, the question of what one is doing when one prays is most properly the work of the appreciative consciousness.

Many definitions of prayer are possible. A commonly-accepted one in the Catholic tradition is "lifting one's mind and heart to God." Prayer is always relational and implies that the person engages God. The felt forms of this engagement are many: praise, petition, thanksgiving, contrition, awe.

New forms of prayer are being discovered today. Strongly influenced by the Eastern religions, Christian prayer can incorporate Zen, yoga, or meditative tones. As snow becomes rain, these Eastern forms transmute themselves into Christian forms under faith. The question is, why are these forms so popular? Eastern forms tend characteristically toward the nonrational. They keep the mind's rational function silent. For example, a koan in Zen meditation (e.g., what is the sound of one hand clapping?) is a puzzle designed to frustrate the mind's penchant to work. The fact that the Eastern forms are so actively sought indicates that the Eastern forms provide something lacking in the Western forms. It might suggest that the Western forms are rationalistic. Without straining the differences, we may suggest that Western forms appear active, rational, and doer-oriented; the Eastern forms seem more passive, nonrational, and being-oriented. This dilemma does not imply the bankruptcy of Western prayer forms. The dilemma is not resolved either by substituting Eastern for Western forms or by a synthesis of the two in a syncretism where the loss of both identities occurs. The work of William Johnston on Zen and Anthony de Mello on Sadhana uses Christian tradition in dialogue with Eastern and Hindu forms of prayer similar to what should be done in Western tradition.[30] The flight to the East suggests that a thorough understanding of the Western tradition does not exist. A nonrational approach exists in the Western tradition which needs retrieval. However, simply resuscitating old bones of our spiritual tradition will not be helpful. New flesh from a twentieth-century understanding of consciousness and human person must be added. Thus the bones of retrieval become enfleshed as revision. Appreciative prayer is one attempt at this revision.[31]

Rooted in Meland's understanding of the human person and the relationship between thinking and feeling, appreciative prayer expresses the lifting of one's feeling to God. In the Western tradition mental prayer

[30] W. Johnston, *The Inner Eye of Love* (San Francisco: Harper & Row, 1978) 13–32; A. de Mello, *Sadhana* (Anand, India: Anand, 1978) 3–5.

[31] The Western tradition of prayer contains the feeling-dimension which needs representation in the sense of Tracy's revisionist model. The mystics are one group receiving study today, but other areas such as devotions in the wider cultural context should not be ignored. If one takes seriously that the *lex orandi* is the *lex credendi*, shifting prayer forms suggest a change in consciousness and theological concerns.

suggests lifting one's mind to God and the feelings trail along. In appreciative prayer the opposite dynamic is at work: one lifts one's feelings to God and the mind trails along.

The use of reason in mental prayer is called discursive prayer. Like a cursor, which is a flashing box on a computer screen that roams around on command to tell us where we are, discursive prayer roams around thinking about the subject matter. Often discursive prayer is taught as introductory prayer and considered as a less mature form of prayer. Mature forms of prayer are quiet forms which stop the hyperactivity of the mind. The prayer of quiet or simplicity rests in the presence of God without a surplusage of thinking. The final phase of mental prayer is contemplative prayer, where God does the communicating. Whereas some people hold contemplation as special to a few monks, ascetics, or mystics, others, like Thomas Merton, suggest that it is possible for all believers.[32] Appreciative prayer agrees with Merton's making contemplation available for all and goes further to provide an option for how prayer is taught and thereby a restatement of the relationship of prayer forms to one another.[33]

Whereas discursive prayer begins with the intellect, appreciative prayer begins in the affectivity of the feelings. Instead of activating the mind as in mental prayer in order to eventually deactivate it, like racing a motor before shutting it off, appreciative prayer resembles contemplative prayer's quiet of the mind in order to pay attention to the feelings. For example, one does not read the Scriptures to think about what Jesus did (discursively); one reads the passage and lets the feelings about Jesus and the people emerge. Acts of praise, thanks, contrition, and love follow along. One gives vent to the feelings touched by the Scriptures. Since I bring myself as I am to the prayer, unresolved problems, tiredness, excitement, or concerns enter into my reading. One acknowledges the feelings and listens to any interior movements from the Lord. Perhaps one feels ashamed, confused, frustrated, depressed, or angry. Above all, the person attends to the presence of God, who interacts upon me through the feelings. The feeling-dimension of my prayer is real communication of the interrelationship between my self and God.

Reason is not discarded in appreciative prayer. Appreciative conscious-

---

[32] T. Merton, *Seeds of Contemplation* (London: Burns and Oates, 1949) 15.

[33] I have a more thorough treatment of "mental" prayer as a historical phenomenon and its relationship to a richer Western tradition of prayer forms, including appreciative prayer compared to Ignatius of Loyola's concern for feelings in prayer, in "Appreciative Prayer and the Mental Prayer Tradition," *Contemplative Review* 15, no. 4 (winter 1982) 1–15. Similarities of appreciative prayer and the concern for feelings in John of the Cross, Teresa of Avila, Meister Eckhart, and the author of the *Cloud of Unknowing* would also be beneficial for a revisionist theology of prayer.

ness begins in open awareness toward my self, world, God, and then moves progressively through the feelings to the identification of the self and God in relationship. Then it discriminates the mutual feeling tone of the intercommunication, e.g., joy, peace, anger, thanks. Constant testing through the discernment of spirits is necessary to determine whether my feelings are accurately related to God. The rational consciousness correlates the feeling and meaning of that feeling.

Appreciative prayer is not at odds with discursive prayer but represents another approach to prayer. For busy people in the Western tradition, quiet attention to feelings toward husband, wife, children, job, events, the Church, and my self are extremely important and a source of Christian nourishment. Hence the feelings that I bring are not a distraction but something important to my total presence before the Lord. Appreciative prayer allows the feelings which undergird my busyness to ebb and flow before the Lord. As I pray, acts of praise, thanksgiving, adoration, and love are encouraged responses which call me to a conversion of my feelings related to God, others, and self.

Teaching people to pray need not begin with an emphasis upon the mind. Teaching people to begin by quieting down the mind resembles the mode of contemplative prayer and is the approach of appreciative prayer. Appreciative prayer is not infused but is acquired through gradual skilling analogous to aesthetic skill. The feeling-dimension of religious experience is worked on and listened to and used for a better life.

Prayer cannot be viewed in isolation from the rest of life. Prayer seems to be a natural outpouring of the human person, and it would seem a truism that people pray because they are human. The function of prayer within the wider sphere of human experience is crucial to prayer itself and to the human person who prays. At least three tensions exist for human experience that pours into prayer: the rational and appreciative modes, the individual and community, knowledge and love. These tensions should be examined both from the perspective of discursive and appreciative prayer and within Western tradition. While appreciative prayer forms only will be examined, I believe they more adequately incorporate the natural tensions within prayer than other forms.

First, a healthy tension exists between the rational and the appreciative consciousness. For Western culture, elevating the rational mode to exclude the appreciative is the greater danger. Prayer becomes lifeless, without feeling, and without love expressed. Likewise, elevating the appreciative mode to exclude the rational mode can also be a danger. God grants insight through the rational mode too. Correlating the two is the key, so that they complement one another. At one time discursive prayer will be appealing, at another time appreciative prayer. The person determines which is best suited for the occasion.

While a person is praying, the appreciative mode is in ascension and leads the encounter. If the rational mode enters in the form of an analysis, attention to the other (God) is blocked, with the result that I would be restricting God's communication. The person must first pay attention to the mutually engaging relationship which not only listens but prompts one to praise, remain silent, become affectionate, or seek reconciliation. Attention to the encounter, and thereby to the encountered one, which moves the person to expressed acts of love, is the hallmark of appreciative prayer.

Prayer is fundamentally relational. It is related not only to God but to my whole life context, which includes the choices made, the options preferred, the hopes, failures, and values held. Thus, like waves against the beach, appreciative prayer ebbs in from the cultural relationships that comprise my life and flows out again from my faith: I pray in good times with praise and thanksgiving and in bad times with petition and acceptance. On a particular day one mood may be prevalent and I cannot ignore it. For example, I may be angry, lonely, tired, or sick when I pray. I do not pretend that my context and my feeling toward it are not influencing my praying; for without attention to the wholeness of the encounter, which is best grasped by the appreciative mode, prayer becomes disconnected from living, or worse, it becomes an escape from God's call to conversion.

A second tension exists between the individual and the community. Individualized prayer runs the risk of self-centering the person, with the result that prayer does not expand to include others and thereby constricts the self. In our Western culture the emphasis upon freedom and the individual accentuates the drive toward individualism. Hence people find communal prayer distracting and difficult to participate in. For example, to those whose prayer is individualized, Eucharistic liturgies which ask for participation can become a threat and not really be prayer. The question is not one of substituting one pole, the community, for the other, individual, such that private prayer is old-fashioned, but of allowing the two to interpenetrate each other.

The principle of appreciative prayer is individual-in-community: if one prays in private, one should bring his or her relationality to others; if one prays in common, the wholeness of the group accentuates the individual's part. For example, when I pray alone, I allow my feelings toward people and events to ebb-flow into my prayer as I bring myself before the Lord. I encourage the prayerfulness of these feelings by acts of praise and thanksgiving for these relationships and ask that they may become salvific for me and others. In the same way, when I pray in common, I do not assert my individual prayer but unite myself with the community. I allow commonly recited prayers, the Amen, singing, actions, to express my own affective praise and thanksgiving, hopes and petitions. In this way I become an active part of the whole by feeling into the situation and letting it be my prayer. The form may not be individualized, but my participation seals the action as mine. Appreciative prayer does not make a bad sermon good nor does it pretend it is worse than it is: appreciative prayer permits the limitations of the sermon to touch me where it can and I listen with ear and feelings to what might be gained. Each communal prayer demands greater or lesser participation and response. Through attention to the feeling-dimension, appreciative prayer finds private and communal prayer two inextricable poles of the same activity mutually informing each other.

A third healthy tension in prayer is between knowledge and love. The interrelationship of the two is the key. In our examination of the natural relationship between faith and appreciative awareness, we determined that faith directs the self toward love, and appreciative awareness yields knowledge of the heart. In appreciative prayer the faith dimension directs the appreciative awareness toward love of God; in turn, appreciative awareness extracts a knowledge born of love which allows a richer, deeper love. As reflective analysis, the rational consciousness should enter only after prayer is finished in order to discriminate what I did, how I felt, the way I reacted, and thereby hone my appreciative skill in prayer. Otherwise one is doing discursive prayer.

Faith orchestrates and directs these three tensions toward deeper love. God's grace comes to me as an empowerment which continually centers my life in His. This energy of grace is psychic, social, and redemptive and is experienced as forgiveness and a love beyond my possession. In appreciative prayer one turns completely toward God in open awareness in order to allow the intercommunication of love. Thus the conversation is not forced, but one speaks or listens depending upon which is beckoned forth. One watches and listens to the mutuality of the relationship with the eyes and ears of the heart. The response is signaled by the pressure, the pain, the pining, the wooing, and the desire for deeper love, which becomes expressed affectively throughout the prayer as one is inclined. This appreciative prayer seeking God might best be characterized as suffering love: both in the sense of desiring deeper and more complete loving union and in the sense of falling short of total love in this limited world.

Appreciative prayer is only one example of the pastoral application of Meland's central theological insights. Worship, ritual, symbols, sacraments, and devotions are other areas of immediate application. My own pastoral experience leads me to conclude that in moral decision-making the feeling-dimension is a more basic context than rational analysis. At the same time, I certainly hold the importance of intellectual conversion and its power upon feelings. Yet the feeling-dimension orients reason and reinforces moral choices. Even when reason dictates the principles to be followed, the feeling-dimension exhibits the extent and depth of the commitment. One cannot profess Christ with the lips; one must live it in one's heart. The work of theology should include articulations of the feeling-dimension in belief as a way of knowing. Meland has made an important and timely contribution from the American perspective for integrating our life today.

Let me offer one final consideration. The feeling-dimension of religious experience suggests that Christian living itself might also be understood as an art. The Christian is sent to others to help them find God's presence. Life reflects our process of growth as it is fitted to temperament, circumstances, choices, obstacles, successes, and aspirations. I am not referring merely to biological life, but life united to God which understands a world moving in creative passage that seeks deeper love of Him. For humanity's sake, we will not allow islands to be mistaken for isolated bodies of land and thereby cheapen our response to God as individuals-in-community. Life is too precious. Christian faith searches to transform life for the benefit of all, so that the love of God, love of neighbor, and love of creation become one interconnected act of love.

INDEX OF NAMES

INDEX OF TOPICS

146

GEORGETOWN UNIVERSITY PRESS
STUDIES IN ETHICS Series